The Credit Jungle

A Consumers' Guide to Credit

by
Robert Dietz
&
Michael Langer

JAIN PUBLISHING COMPANY
Fremont, California

Although the authors have used due diligence to ensure the accuracy and completeness of the information contained in this book, all content is to be viewed as general information only and should not be construed as actual legal, accounting or financial advice of a personal nature. The ideas, suggestions, general principles and conclusions presented in this book may be subject to further local, state and federal laws and regulations. The continually changing economic and political environment could possibly demand reinterpretation of some or all of the concepts presented herein. Readers should consult a licensed professional for their specific situations. Neither the author nor the publisher assume any liability for any errors, omissions or inaccuracies.

Library of Congress Cataloging-in-Publication Data

Dietz, Robert, 1955-
    The credit jungle : a consumers' guide to credit / by Robert Dietz & Michael Langer.
       p.   cm.
   ISBN 0-87573-069-8
   1. Consumer credit.   2. Credit cards.   I. Langer, Michael, 1946- .   II. Title.
HG3755.D5   1995
332.7'43—dc20   95-11720
                                    CIP

Contents

Introduction

Everyone has heard the phrase "it's a jungle out there," and it rings especially true in today's credit society. Credit is a necessity in most of our daily lives, and pity the person who doesn't believe it. Whenever we're buying anything anywhere the phrase we never fail to hear is "Will that be cash or charge?" Although most of us can buy the small, everyday things we need with cash we quickly find out we need credit to purchase the larger, more expensive items. Without credit our choices are severely limited and many of the things we aspire to own, such as a nice car or home, will probably remain out of reach.

What is CREDIT and why would you ever need it? Let's start small and work our way up. The last time you were in the mall and saw that state of the art computer or the perfect diamond tennis bracelet you wanted you had some immediate decisions to make . . . whether to make the purchases and how to pay for them. Without credit you either have to have the cash on hand or get ready to save for what you want.

Now imagine seeing those items and knowing you MUST HAVE THEM NOW. You take out your charge card, give it to the clerk and the items become yours. You will pay for them later. This is the magic of credit and the reason why everyone wants it: being able to go where you want or buy what you need without paying until later.

Credit is not a luxury accorded to only a few but a NECESSITY EVENTUALLY NEEDED BY EVERYONE. You must remember that it is never too early nor too late to get your credit established. Anyone with a source of income and a place of residence is eligible for credit consideration.

Credit is what this book is all about. You won't be bored with a lot of unimportant facts and figures; you will be shown how to establish and keep a good credit history. You will also learn how to overcome obstacles that could prevent you from having the good credit you deserve. YOU NEED THIS BOOK IF YOU: are concerned about your ability to obtain credit; are concerned about your current credit situation; need to clean up or remove erroneous data from your credit report; are a married female contemplating divorce; are a single woman contemplating marriage; have bill collectors contacting you; have a concern about medical bills tarnishing your credit; are currently behind in paying your bills; are considering bankruptcy; or just want to know what to do should you find yourself in any of these situations.

By following the procedures in this book, you can achieve the good credit you desire, but you have to put forth the initiative. It may appear difficult but, by being persistent, it can be done. The choice is yours.

So read on and learn how to become a responsible member of, and succeed in, THE CREDIT JUNGLE.

1

Establishing Credit

Remember the last time you were waiting in line to pay for your $19.95 sweater and the person in front of you took out a wallet full of credit cards? He selected one and paid for his hundreds of dollars worth of clothes. He probably had less than the $30 cash you were holding, but he had the ability to buy practically anything he wanted with all those credit cards. Wouldn't it be great to have that kind of freedom?! How do YOU get it?

You begin by establishing your credit. This won't be easily accomplished because most creditors are hesitant to take a chance on a person with no credit history. The key, however, is PERSISTENCE. While trying to get your credit started you'll probably be turned down more than just once. When this happens, don't get discouraged . . . just apply somewhere else. Everyone has different criteria for extending credit, and eventually someone is going to extend credit to you. Your persistence will pay off.

Offers of credit will probably not initially come to you; you'll have to take the first step. By setting up your credit history now you will avoid problems, and possibly embarrassment, in the future. So why wait?

Once you've made the commitment to begin establishing your credit, you'll need to know where to begin. The following pages will cover many possible institutions where you can apply for credit. Let's begin now.

Credit Cards

CREDIT CARDS are, simply, plastic money. They allow you to receive service or merchandise now and pay for it later. Your payments will be determined by the type of card you have and your credit limit.

Practically every major bank, department store and oil company offers credit cards. There are in excess of 25,000 different ones available to consumers, and the list is growing. There are almost as many different fees and interest rates as there are credit cards, so it is important to SHOP AROUND when applying for your first credit card. If at first you're turned down for one, apply for another. Keep applying until you're successful.

Oil Companies

Not long ago, credit cards issued by oil companies were only good for gasoline and auto repairs. With the emergence of gasoline mini-marts these cards have become more desirable. A consumer can now get anything from tires to groceries to film at the "gas station." Naturally, because of this diversification, the demand for oil company cards has grown.

All major oil companies and many of the smaller ones issue credit cards. The competition among the companies is so great that the standards for obtaining their cards are less stringent than with other industries. By extending credit to qualified "first-timers," the oil companies are assured of their card holders loyalty to their products. In fact, many people who have credit already established will tell you that their first line of credit was from an oil company, and that they continue to use that companys products.

The goods and services that you charge are billed monthly and, depending upon the company, you may be required to pay the entire amount or a minimum payment each month. These payments must be made on time because failure to do so may result in the company reporting the delinquency to the credit bureau, where all other oil companies will know of your poor payment history and you will probably have a difficult time receiving other oil cards.

Single Purpose Cards

A SINGLE PURPOSE CARD is one that is issued by a specific company and that will be honored only by that company and its affiliates. Major hotels, airlines, and even telephone companies issue them, but the most common single purpose card is offered by retail department stores.

There are almost as many different department store credit cards as there are department stores. The best place to start your quest for a single purpose credit card is not necessarily at one of the larger retail stores but rather at a smaller one. Remember the competition we spoke of among oil companies? It's just as fierce among the many smaller retail stores. This makes their cards easier to obtain. Shop around your own neighborhood shopping centers and malls and you'll be surprised at the number of smaller stores that will issue their own line of credit. Their leniency in extending first-timers credit assures them of loyalty.

This is not to say that the larger stores will not extend credit. These days, many of the more well known retailers are bombarding customers entering their stores with offers of limited days interest free and other enticements. Again, because of the competition factor, if you are credit worthy, it is a good bet that you can obtain one of these cards.

Remember not to get discouraged if you're turned down at first; keep applying and stick to the retail stores in the areas of greatest competition for the best results. You'll eventually achieve success.

Bank Cards

BANK CARDS are credit cards issued by practically all financial institutions. The two most common ones are VISA and MASTERCARD, and the competition between the two is fierce. Every major bank, as well as many other lending institutions, offer these two cards. It is the responsibility of the issuer to determine which of their applicants is extended credit. They must also determine at what interest rates and credit limits the credit is granted, so it's best to shop around for the best offers. Each institution also sets its own criteria for rating a credit application, so if one place denies you credit, apply elsewhere (See Chapter 2).

Bank cards are becoming increasingly popular because of the wide variety of places and ways they can be used. They allow you to order things by phone and, in some states, even pay speeding tickets. They can be used at gas stations, grocery stores, and fast food establishments, and are even accepted for payment of taxes, movies, parking garages, and phone calls.

Secured Cards and Debit Cards

The best kind of bank card for a first timer to obtain is one that is not available everywhere. This is called the SECURED CARD, which is a Visa or Mastercard with special restrictions. The idea here is to open a savings account at an institution with a minimum balance which is set by them. They will then issue you a credit card using your savings account to secure your purchases. Your credit limit will be a percentage of your account balance, so you will not be able to withdraw money from the account without jeopardizing your credit allowance.

The money in the account is still your money and it will accrue interest at advertised rates. However, the interest charged on the card is usually a little higher than for non-secured cards.

If you don't have the necessary amount of money to obtain a secured card, ask your friends or relatives to loan it to you. There is little risk for them because you won't be spending the money; it will be bearing interest for them as if they had deposited the money in their own account. When the money becomes available, they will have more than their initial investment.

These cards are ideal not only for first-timers wanting to establish credit, but also for persons wanting to re-establish their credit after problems have tarnished their history. If you follow the requirements of paying on time, most institutions will eventually upgrade your credit status to non-secured.

Check your own bank first to see if they offer secured cards. Many times they will issue you their bank card on a secured basis, even if that is not their normal policy, rather than risk losing you as a customer. If they do not, look in you local newspapers for advertised institutions that do offer the service, but check out the offer thoroughly before accepting it. Remember, however, that it is the individual institutions that will determine who is eligible, so if you're turned down, try somewhere else. You should beware of services that charge a fee for secured cards. That fee is only to pass on your application, which you can do for free.

DEBIT CARDS are cards that are linked directly to your checking account, and your credit limit is determined by your account balance. Funds are taken out of your checking account so there is no monthly bill; be sure to keep track of all transactions so as not to overdraw your account.

As with secured cards, these are not very common, so it is best to check with your bank to see if they offer debit cards. Keep in mind, however, that since they are linked directly with your checking account, if you have a history of bouncing checks, you may not be eligible. If they don't, check the media (See Chapter 12 for more information).

Travel and Entertainment Cards (T & E Cards)

These cards differ from bank cards by catering foremost to business people and frequent travelers. They have rigid criteria that must be met before they are issued. Annual fees are charged for the privilege of carrying these cards. In return, you get a higher line of credit and additional benefits not offered by bank cards. Along with the higher credit limit comes the requirement to PAY THE BALANCE IN FULL EACH MONTH. There is no interest charge but there may be a late charge should your monthly payoff be late.

Although the criteria for obtaining these cards has been eased somewhat due to their increased popularity, Travel and Entertainment cards are still among the most difficult to get; avoid applying for these until a strong credit history is established. The most common T&E cards are AMERICAN EXPRESS, DINERS CLUB and CARTE BLANCHE.

Premium Bank Cards

PREMIUM BANK CARDS, as with T&E cards, cater to the credit elite . . . that group of people with a good credit history and above average income. These cards are usually issued by invitation of the lending institution.

The most common premium cards are the GOLD VISA and MASTERCARD. These differ from T&E cards in that there may not be an annual fee, the balance is not due in full at the end of each month, and, although they do have an interest rate, it is generally lower than for regular bank cards. As with T&E cards, the credit limit is higher. Many of the benefits offered to T&E cardholders are offered to premium bank card holders, and, again, competition between these and T&E cards is great, so the issuers are always coming up with new ideas and perks to entice new members.

Loans

Applying for a loan is a good way to establish credit. Banks, savings and loans and finance companies are some of the institutions that give loans. Your first stop should be the place where you do your banking. If you're denied a loan there go someplace else.

Bank loans are usually more difficult to get approved than loans at finance companies. Banks have more stringent criteria requiring an applicant to have some established credit and enough assets to collateralize the requested loan amount. Assets can be car titles, stock certificates, property deeds or savings accounts. A cosigner to your loan may also be required to put up collateral. Banks stress income as an important factor in determining loan approval.

Banks offer lower interest rates and higher loan limits than finance companies, and they are definitely harder to obtain. If you have no established credit, a finance company will be a better starting place.

FINANCE COMPANIES deal mainly with loans, and although the interest rates are generally higher and loan amounts lower, the applications are much less complicated and demanding than those required by banks. Many take initial applications for loans over the phone. Additionally, your application can be approved or denied within hours. Cosigners are usually not needed. If approved, your check could be ready within a day. Some allow loans to be collateralized through household possessions such as TV's, stereos and computers. You pay more for your loan and development of your credit history, but we are recommending methods that will heighten your chances for success. In addition, by making your monthly payments on time, you should have little trouble securing future loans from that particular institution. Finance companies do require an applicant to be honest, have a steady income and a history of residential and employment stability.

In the preceding paragraphs we've mentioned cosigners. A few additional words are necessary on this term. A COSIGNER is another person who will take the responsibility for repayment of the loan should you default on your agreement. A cosigner must be employed with a steady income and prior credit already established. Good cosigners include parents, siblings and very good friends; people who know you well enough to realize you won't renege on your payments.

Credit Unions

CREDIT UNIONS are cooperative associations designed to provide members with a place to save money and obtain low interest loans. Some also issue low interest bank cards. Many businesses use credit unions, and employees of those companies can deposit money into their checking and savings account directly from their paychecks. The accumulated savings can be used at any time or can be used as collateral for loans.

Applying for a loan at a CU is easy; there is little red tape involved. Loan amounts can vary from a couple of hundred dollars to many thousands of dollars, with the decision concerning approval being made swiftly. Repayment terms can be as long as five years for unsecured loans, possibly as high as ten years if secured.

Ask your employer if your company uses a credit union. If they do, become a member. Every member of a credit union is also considered one of its owners, but the CU is not in business to make money. For this reason, interest rates on loans and credit cards can be held to a minimum. CU's are an excellent alternative to banks and finance companies. They can be a valuable asset in your quest to establish credit.

Automobile Financing

Another way to establish credit is by buying a car. The easiest way is to enlist the aid of a qualified cosigner. With one, most car dealers will not deny credit to a first time buyer. We'll admit that there are places that will offer financing to someone with no credit established, but you'll spend valuable time looking, and then end up paying higher finance charges. Ask someone to cosign and you can practically guarantee the car will be yours. Just be sure to keep up with your payments because how you pay will also have an effect on your cosigner's credit rating.

Loans by Mail

Look in the classified section of any major newspaper or check-out counter tabloid and you'll see many ads for loans by mail. Many of these ads, although worded differently, are identical; they're set up under different company names but run by the same individuals. When you request information through the ads many of the reply letters will be the same. They will send you a short application which you are required to return along with A FEE. They claim to be able to SECURE A LOAN FOR YOU REGARDLESS OF YOUR CREDIT HISTORY. What you actually get for your money is a list of places where you can apply for loans, many of which can be found in the yellow pages. Replies to your requests may take forever. Results are usually much less than promised. Attempts to get your filing fee returned after you get no results are basically futile. You'll end up spending valuable time and money for few, if any, results. While a few of these ads may actually help you, the majority will not. In fact, many states are now aggressively searching for and prosecuting the people who run these loan by mail scams (See Chapter 12). STAY AWAY FROM THESE ADS!!!

Students and Credit

Many institutions are now targeting students with offers of credit cards because of the huge market that exists. High school seniors and college students alike are being bombarded with offers though most have no means of income. The creditors are betting that this group presents no greater risk than that of the average consumer, gambling that parents will feel a moral obligation to "bail out" their children even though they bear no legal obligation to do so.

Loyalty is also a major reason for this marketing push. Allowing students to obtain their first major credit card might secure the students allegiance to the creditor in the future, after graduation. Handled properly, this first credit can make it easier to obtain future credit . . . but, there are pitfalls.

Many students will end up quitting school and be forced to work full-time to pay off their debt. Many will incur great debt by the time they graduate, forcing them into counselling or bankruptcy. Students, especially high school seniors who may have had no curriculum on credit awareness, have no idea of the responsibility involved in having a credit card, and since the offers are flying in, they may receive many cards at once, setting themselves up for disaster.

Although the credit limits are low, students and parents alike may be in for a rude introduction into the world of credit. If you are a student, learn what you can about credit responsibility and discuss the situation with your parents. If you do decide to obtain a credit card, use it wisely and it may lead to better things in the future.

In summation, remember to BE PERSISTENT when applying for first time credit. DON'T GET DISCOURAGED by a couple of rejections. SHOP AROUND for the best rates on bank cards and stick to the areas of greatest competition for department store cards. If possible, become a member of a credit union where it is easier to apply for a loan, and, by all means, AVOID THOSE LOAN BY MAIL SCAMS.

2

The Credit Application

Now that you know where to apply for credit you need to know what to expect from the credit applications you must complete. Certain requirements must be met before you're extended credit, but lenders are generally concerned with 3 things when determining credit worthiness: ability to repay, past credit history, and collateral. Specific types of questions are inapplicable and illegal on applications. Always read the fine print of any application or contract that you sign; it will assist in helping you understand the specifics of the credit you may receive. Depending upon the type of credit you're applying for, the application may vary in length and request for details, but certain criteria are always required, whether you're applying for a mortgage or a credit card.

Criteria for Credit Approval

The most important determinate of receiving credit is your income. It must be from a steady source and large enough to enable you to pay your debts.

Certain occupations are considered better risks than others in obtaining credit. Those that offer advancement opportunity, entry level, professional and managerial positions are considered good risks. Occupations on the other side of the spectrum are those whose income is derived primarily from tips or commission and those paying minimum wage. However, since every institution sets its own standards, you may get credit extended to you even though you fall into one of the bad risk occupational groups. The key is to keep applying until you get what you need.

There are exceptions to bad risk occupations. If you are a female who relies on alimony or child support, or a dependent of someone who already has credit established, you may be eligible to receive credit even if you are in a bad risk occupation.

The length of time you've been on your job is also important. Job stability is sought by creditors. The worst thing to show a potential creditor is that you have a history of job hopping. You may hate your job, but stick with it until you have established credit; you can always leave once you get your credit established. If you haven't been at your job too long, but feel a good rapport with your employer, ask him/her to verify your job at a longer length of service and at a higher income. Be certain to discuss what you want your employer to say so you avoid conflicting stories. You may also include part time work on your application if you have sufficient time in on the job, but make sure it is verifiable. It can't hurt.

A bank account (checking or savings) is another important piece of criteria looked at by the reviewing creditor. If you don't have a bank account, open one up before you apply for credit. It shows the creditor that you can save money and avoid wild spending habits. Open the account at the bank where you'll be applying for credit. Even if the bank denies you credit, keep the account active to show on future credit applications.

As we mentioned earlier, stability at your place of residence is important. If you have address changes due to job transfers, tell the creditors; it should have no bearing on your ability to get credit. If you've recently moved, your previous long term address will show stability.

Renters who have been at their same address for a good length of time are believed to be stable, responsible persons. If you don't have a permanent residence, don't apply for credit. Using a P.O. Box or hotel as your place of residence will surely lead to credit denial.

Other positive factors include having monthly bills amounting to less than half your monthly income, the number of dependents you have and, of course, the contents of your credit report.

These are some of the criteria that creditors will consider to determine whether or not you are credit worthy. Keep in mind that each institution sets its own criteria. Again, if one place turns you down apply at another one. PERSISTENCE PAYS OFF.

What Creditors Can't Ask

According to the EQUAL CREDIT OPPORTUNITY ACT, the creditor can only ask questions relating to your credit history and ability to pay your bills. Any questions that deal with race, religion, sexual preference or national origin are discriminatory and need not be answered. You cannot be denied credit for refusing to answer such questions. If you've been refused credit for reasons you believe are discriminatory, complain to the institution where you applied. If you receive no satisfaction, consider registering a complaint against them with the Federal Trade Commission.

The Equal Credit Opportunity Act also makes it illegal to deny credit because of sex. Read more on this in Chapter 6.

Scoring the Application

As we've stated, every institution has its own system for scoring the credit application. One of the most widely used is the Point System, which issues points when key requirements are met. You must receive the minimum number necessary for approval. As an example, the longer you've been on your job the more points you are awarded.

All the criteria previously mentioned will be evaluated and assigned a certain number of points. The total number awarded to the completed application will determine whether or not you qualify for credit. Each creditor determines the point amounts needed for credit approval and how the criteria are to be weighed. Remember that your application answers will be verified, so either be truthful or consistent in your responses and let others know how you responded if they are to verify your answers (such as employer,landlord, etc.). A lie on your application may result in denial of credit.

There are also "hit or miss" institutions, who receive so many applications for credit on a regular basis that their reviews of each application are scant. They don't bother to verify all the information on an application, which results in some being approved in a rather arbitrary fashion. It also leads to applications being denied for less than excellent reasons. Many of these places are set up on quotas, and the reviewer is required to complete a specified number of applications a day, and therefore just skims them. We suggest that an initial denial by one of these creditors not stop you from reapplying at a later date.

Some creditors will score the application based on comparisons with other customers. They look at information on your credit report (how close are your charge card balances to the limits, purchases, lates, etc.) and compare it to other existing customers to determine the risk factor. This is a common type ofscoring when the creditor is considering giving a limit increase.

Many businesses will base their decision totally on the content of your credit report, with the bureau scoring the credit report based on all of the information contained on it. It is not widely used, but it is increasing in popularity as a tool for creditors. We will cover credit reports in detail in Chapter 5.

Finally, there may just be a time when someone will extend credit to you just because of the way you presented yourself. It's very important to appear self confident when speaking to a potential creditor. If you act in a mature fashion and show that you have good character, getting your credit may be easier than you thought.

A Word About Interest Rates

The INTEREST RATE is a fee that is added to any unpaid balance of your bill. The rate may vary from place to place and is usually a percentage of the credit limit or loan amount. You should always shop around and look for the lowest interest rate available on credit lines or loans. A law recently enacted, called The Truth in Lending Act, requires issuers of credit to print, on credit applications, applicable interest rates, making it easier to shop around.

An even better way to shop and compare is by checking the annual percentage rate, or APR. The APR is the cost of the credit on a yearly basis, converted into a percentage, and includes not only interest but other costs such as application fees, handling fees, credit report fees, points, appraisal fees, and other charges. The CONSUMER CREDIT PROTECTION ACT makes it mandatory that the APR is disclosed, in large type, on all loan agreements.

Most lending institutions make their money through interest rates and other charges, which is why smaller institutions, with less capital to work with, will usually charge higher interest rates.

Reasons for Denial

When you first start applying for credit you will probably be denied at least once. You must learn why you have been denied so that you can take corrective measures to avoid future denials. Creditors denying an application for credit MUST inform you, in writing, of their reasons. Their response to you is usually within a thirty day period from your date of application. If you are dissatisfied with the reasons given, approach the creditor and question them about their denial. You have a right to investigate the reason for denial, free of charge, so take advantage of it.

There are any number of reasons why your application for credit may be refused. The length of time on your job, or the job itself may be a reason for denial. If length of service is the problem ask your employer to verify a longer employment time. If the job is the problem, think up different, more acceptable names for it and reapply. If salary is the problem, ask your employer to verify it at a higher rate, but remember, ONLY APPLY FOR AS MUCH CREDIT AS YOU CAN COMFORTABLY AFFORD TO REPAY.

Other reasons include an insufficient length of time at your place of residence, prior filing of bankruptcy or judgments against you from other creditors (doctors, landlords, hospitals, etc). Simply having no credit, or bad credit, may, in itself, be used as reason for denying you credit.

Finally, just applying for too many credit cards or other forms of credit within a limited amount of time may result in denial of credit. Each time you apply for credit, the creditor will have to order a copy of your credit report. Every request may show up as an inquiry. Too many inquiries within a limited period of time give the prospective creditors the impression that you might be planning on overextending yourself with credit purchases. They view a flood of applications as being indicative of a financial problem. Space your applications over at least a 30 day period.

Do not get discouraged over a credit denial. The creditors who deny you credit are required to inform you of the reason in writing, so learn what you need to do to make yourself a better credit risk. Many people who now have credit established were denied at least once when they first began their credit quest. Creditors can't make money by denying applications. BE PERSISTENT. When you get your first application approved all the disappointment you went through will quickly be forgotten.

Pre-Approved Applications

Some companies will send out "pre-approved" applications in an effort to get more people to apply for their credit. Thousands and thousands are mailed at one time so you should know that they all cannot be pre-approved. Don't assume that just because you complete and mail in one of these applications that you are assured of getting credit. The application will usually go through the same approval process that we discussed earlier, and you may still be denied credit.

DO NOT APPLY FOR CREDIT IF YOU AREN'T 100% CERTAIN THAT YOU CAN HANDLE THE RESPONSIBILITY. Many people get themselves into horrible situations because they become credit crazy, overextend themselves, and fail to budget their money properly. If you can honestly say that you are ready to accept responsibility for entering into a controlled indebtedness, then go for it.

If you're not sure you're ready, wait. There's plenty of time to enter into the world of credit without going into uncontrolled debt. Use your head; use your credit wisely.

3

Your Credit History

Congratulations. You've persevered in your quest and you've been awarded your first line of credit. What do you do now? How do you handle this new responsibility? First, sit back, relax and savor the moment. As long as you meet your payment obligations the hard part is over. Stop applying for credit for a while and let this first line of credit work for you; there'll be more to come in the future. Just take it one step at a time.

Your credit history has now officially begun. This is the information upon which other creditors will base your future extensions of credit. It is your ability and willingness to pay your bills when they are due and in the amount required by your agreements and arrangements. A good credit history is your assurance that if you want or need something you'll be able to get it. IT'S YOUR TICKET TO ADDITIONAL CREDIT.

People frequently confuse credit rating with credit history, but the two are distinctly different. A CREDIT RATING is how a current creditor rates your payment history. Your CREDIT HISTORY is a compilation of all your reported credit experiences, and ALL POTENTIAL CREDITORS WILL REVIEW IT when determining your eligibility to possess their credit. How you use your credit and your payment habits are essential to the development and continuation of a good credit history. Start it off good from the beginning and take care of it.

Using Your New Credit

How you use your credit will have significant impact on potential creditors. Loans are usually obtained for a specific purpose such as a vacation or major purchase. Even if you wanted the loan for the singular purpose of establishing your credit, the creditor has no way to track the use of the money. Observe this caution: always use the loan for the purpose cited on your loan application. Should the creditor discover that the loan was used for other than its intended purpose (although this would be quite difficult) he could declare the agreement void and demand payment in full. In extreme circumstances legal action could result against you or your cosigner.

The information reflected on your credit report when you use a credit card is significantly more extensive than that which describes your creditors' opinions of your loan activities. When you receive a credit card, the accompanying agreement describes your credit and cash advance limits. YOU MUST AVOID THE PERIODIC TEMPTATION TO EXCEED THESE LIMITS; if you do not you will begin to show a pattern that creditors may interpret as wild and heavy spending. Such a pattern can jeopardize future attempts to obtain additional credit.

When you exceed the preset limits on your charge card you will be expected to pay, in full, any excess amount. Should an emergency arise during that time you won't be able to use your credit to help you through it. When you use your card wisely and stay within your credit limits, you'll be able to use it when you need it. Additionally, your payments will remain minimal and will easily fit into your budget, or you may wish to pay your smaller balances in full to avoid paying the interest.

Remember that not all stores will check your credit card limit through its issuing office. This means that if you have reached your limit on the card a store may improperly allow you to exceed it by not calling the sale into the central office. If you don't keep track of how much you've charged you may be unpleasantly surprised when you are billed for much more than the monthly amount you expected. By not being attentive to your charge amounts you may end up in trouble and be referred to collections if you can't pay the unexpected monthly bill.

Use your first credit card for necessities; don't go credit crazy. As with any new line of credit, you'll have to adjust your budget to cover the new payment obligations. Again, we caution you not to keep applying for more and more credit. Each time you're extended additional credit, you have to reorganize your budget to make room for the payments. You can only stretch your budget so far before it collapses. Keep things simple in the beginning; you can apply for more credit when you get used to this initial responsibility. Don't cut yourself short. Remember: THE MORE CREDIT YOU HAVE, THE MORE MONEY YOU NEED TO BUDGET AWAY TO MAKE THE PAYMENTS.

Credit Card Fraud

Another way to take care of your new credit is to protect yourself against credit fraud, which has become a growing problem. Con artists are preying on innocent people, getting them to reveal their credit card numbers, stealing statements from the mail or personal information from the trash, then selling the information, running up unauthorized charges or applying for fraudulent loans to the tune of hundreds of millions of dollars each year.

Ways that you can protect yourself include knowing what you charge. Keep your receipts and compare them to the bills you receive. Report any charges that aren't yours to the bank IMMEDIATELY and close the account. You should also notify the bank if you don't receive a new card or a monthly statement.

Always sign your credit cards upon receiving them. Keep your card in view at the check-out line. Avoid signing blank receipts and draw lines through any blank spaces above the total. Void and destroy all carbons and incorrect receipts; don't let the store keep them.

Never give your credit card number out over the telephone unless you are dealing with a reputable company. If someone calls you requesting your credit card number, don't give it to them—if they say it's your bank, they should already know your account number. Avoid those post cards that come in the mail that say you've won a prize; all they want is your credit card number.

The Big 3 credit reporting agencies—TransUnion, TRW, and Equifax—are working in tandem to help people who have been the victims of credit fraud, assisting them in contacting creditors and adding a "victim of fraud" statement to the credit report. They have a universal form that is shared among the bureaus, so contact them if you've been victimized (see Chapter 5 for addresses).

Protect yourself against credit card fraud; if something sounds too good to be true, it usually is.

The Credit Report

Potential creditors investigate your financial, and possibly even social and moral history by obtaining a copy of your CREDIT REPORT. These credit biographies are supplied to member creditors through one or more of many CREDIT BUREAUS located throughout the country. The bureaus generally all have similar data, although, as you will learn, the information may not always be up-to-date, complete, or even correct.

The credit report not only lists basic information such as your name and social security number, but every possible bit of information pertaining to your credit. This includes where you've applied for credit, payment history with current and past creditors, bankruptcies, tax and other liens, judgments, write off accounts, repossessions, and accounts placed in collections.

These creditors in waiting can learn everything they need to know from your report to make an informed decision on extending you credit. It is most important that you get your credit history off to a good start and keep it as blemish free as possible. A good report will enhance your chances for future credit. We will cover these reports in depth in Chapter 5.

How to Keep a Good Credit History

The obvious way to keep your credit history looking good is by making your payments on time. Allow sufficient time for mailing so the payment reaches the creditor on or, if possible, before the due date; after all, no one has ever been penalized for paying their bills early. Although creditors usually allow a small grace period before assessing late charges to a bill, if you plan ahead and pay on time you will avoid paying more for the credit you have.

Budget yourself accordingly, especially when you know how much your payments will be, and stay within the budget by avoiding excessive use of your credit card. Open a checking account to hold money that will be used solely to pay bills, thus taking away the temptation to spend it. When the bills come, you can easily write a check and mail it out and save yourself the cost of paying for money orders. If you can't pay your bills immediately when they come in the mail, put them in one place so you do not misplace them by the time you're ready to pay. Always put your account number on your checks and place your check number and date of mailing on your account receipts (you'll learn why in a later chapter).

Many people pay all their bills at the same time each month. This practice is fine as long as you know the total amount you have to pay and have the money available to pay it. If you're not certain what the bill amount will be, don't wait until the last moment to pay. Pay as soon as you get it so you won't run short of money.

If you have extra money remaining from your budgeted amount, it never hurts to send a little more than what the creditor expects, although be sure the money isn't needed elsewhere or you'll end up short.

Remember to avoid wild use of your charge card; such abandon will show up on your credit report. The date your account was opened as well as your credit limit both appear on your record. Reaching your credit limit within a short period of time after its approval will signal prospective creditors to your spending habits and may impact on your future ability to get more credit. BE RESPONSIBLE.

The most important thing to remember in keeping your credit good is to contact your creditor any time a payment will be late or must be skipped for a pay period. Let the creditor know as soon as you know. Emergencies do occur and they occasionally must take precedence over other bills. Don't be afraid to contact the creditor and explain the situation. By contacting a creditor in advance you may be allowed to skip a payment and pay double the following month. You may be allowed to make a partial payment with the balance paid the following month, or pay late with no penalty. Don't wait until the last minute and never wait for the creditor to contact you. Such behavior only signals irresponsibility to him.

Acting in a mature, intelligent fashion will secure the good graces of your creditor. If, however, you make it a habit to request extensions on your payments the creditor may turn against you, and in the event of an actual emergency you'll be out of luck. Use your relationship with your creditor to your advantage, but don't abuse it, because an irate creditor may signal the end of your good credit history (see Chapter 4).

Finally, you should avoid, at all costs, having negative factors appear on your credit report. These factors are explained more fully in Chapter 5.

Improving Your Credit History

Thus far we've been dealing with people who have established credit for the first time. What if you already have credit and it's in a shambles? The sorry condition of your credit history means your chances for new credit extensions are probably zero. What should you do? Contact all your creditors and let them know you want to clear up the problems; tell them you're suffering from a temporary cash flow shortage. Try to work out an arrangement to get your payments lowered until you get back on your feet. If your arrangements call for the balance in full, try to arrange monthly payments or a settlement on the outstanding balance.

A SETTLEMENT is where you're granted the ability to pay a percentage of the total amount owed with the bill being designated as settled in full. Be honest with your creditors about your negative situation and they may agree to work with you. If they do establish an easier method of payment during your difficulties DO NOT DEFAULT ON THE NEW AR-RANGEMENTS.

You may be able to apply for a DEBT CONSOLI-DATION LOAN to help you surface from your indebt-edness. This is a loan that is used to pay off all your outstanding bills, leaving you with only the one monthly loan repayment. This type of loan becomes an excellent choice if you can reach settlements with your creditors. You can then pay them off in full and end your debts. Consolidation loans generally have a longer repayment period so your monthly payments will be smaller. There will, however, be greater inter-est placed on the debt until it is retired.

Some creditors who initially were rigid in their statements of not offering you an easier pay off scheme may soften if you supply them with proof that you attempted to get loans to pay off your debt but were denied.

There is also the nether world of debt elimination choices. The first of these are called debt consolidation companies. Only Consumer Credit Counseling offices, operated in conjunction with area governments, are accepted, by law, by all creditors, and the creditors accept their suggested amounts on how much you can afford to pay. For the location nearest you, call 1-800-388-2227. Other debt consolidation agencies that charge fees for disbursing monthly payments for your bills can be rejected by your creditors. Most creditors will, however, accept small regular payments to no payments at all.

Even though bankruptcy promises people in credit trouble a new life by eliminating their debts, it should only be used as a last resort. As we will discuss later, bankruptcy is not always the smartest way to alleviate debt. Future problems derivative from the bankruptcy may be just as bad as the indebtedness you experienced before the bankruptcy.

Classified ads in most major newspapers are full of offers to help you improve bad credit. Some go so far as to say they can turn your bad credit history around in a matter of days. IGNORE THESE ADS! They prey on people desperate to get out of debt or afraid of going into debt. It takes time and effort to repair bad credit, but it can be accomplished without the so called help of these phonies.

They offer all kinds of gimmicks but all you get is reading material that costs you money that you could put to better advantage. The persons running these ads don't care about you, only your money. You can do what they offer by yourself, saving the money they would charge to pay your creditors. Only you, through your diligent efforts, can improve your credit history and remove the negative remarks on it (see Chapter 12).

Married people also end up in debt, but it's seldom that both spouses end up in debt at the same time. The indebtedness is usually caused by using only one partners credit. If this is your situation, you can use your spouses credit to get you out of debt. Apply for a debt consolidation loan under the name of your spouse and pay off all your bills. DON'T USE THE GOOD CREDIT TO GET FURTHER IN DEBT . . . USE IT TO IMPROVE YOUR SITUATION.

If you are in credit trouble and don't feel ready to re-enter the credit world, you may want to wait and let your credit problems pass through aging. The passage of time will eventually improve your credit history because potential creditors will be less affected by old credit history, and negative items must, by law, be removed from a credit report after the passage of a certain length of time, although sometimes you still need to clean up your credit report before re-entering the credit market. We'll explain how to do this in Chapter 5.

Treat your credit history like your best friend. Avoid going into deep debt which may lead to even larger personal and psychological problems. Learn how to avoid the credit abyss. A good credit history will set you up for bigger and better things in the future and make it hard for potential creditors to deny future requests for credit.

Low Interest Cards

Another good way to take care of your credit is to consolidate balances on high interest charge cards into a low interest account. Since credit is already established, you may be able to obtain a low interest card, although the criteria for acceptance is more stringent than for higher interest cards.

If you have any bankruptcies, tax liens, or judgments, you will more than likely be rejected. If you have no adverse credit, there are some ways to increase your chances of obtaining a low interest credit card:

* Limit your existing debt
* Reduce your account balances
* Limit your open accounts and close dormant accounts
* Limit the number of inquiries on your report
* Maintain stability in residence and employment

Following these guidelines will increase your chances of obtaining a low interest credit card and consolidating balances to avoid paying high interest.

Low interest cards have become popular because of the reduced number of consumers applying for credit cards, but they are not all the same, so be sure to read the fine print. You may even wish to notify the bank that issued your cards and see if they will reduce your interest in exchange for keeping you as a customer.

Are You Heading into Debt?

If any of the following statements apply to you, you may be heading into debt. Corrective steps should be taken immediately to turn the situation around:

* Your charge card balances aren't being reduced.
* You only make minimum payments on your installment loans, and smaller down payments on your purchases.

* Your creditors are reminding you that your payments are past due.
* Your credit card and loan payments use a larger percentage of your income than they should.
* You use cash advances on your credit cards for every day expenses like food and rent.
* You pay for one charge card bill with another charge card.
* You're falling behind on rent and utility bills.
* There isn't enough money in your budget to cover your bills.
* You are living paycheck to paycheck

If one or more of these statements apply to you, you should take steps to turn the situation around. Among them, you should:

* Contact your creditors and try to restructure your payments temporarily
* Rethink your budget
* Try to supplement your income
* Reduce your debt

If the situation is beyond taking the above steps, you should contact the nearest Consumer Credit Counselling office before the situation gets any worse.

4

Dealing With Creditors

Whenever you receive credit, you're left with the responsibility of paying monthly bills. If you use your credit wisely and budget your expenses intelligently you will minimize your problems, but when the unexpected does happen and you're left a little short what should you do?

The first thing to do is to contact any creditor to whom a payment will be skipped or sent in late. As soon as you realize there will be a cash flow problem, call and explain the situation. Every lending institution has an established policy that allows them to negotiate with borrowers who are financially strapped, but most people don't use this service early enough. Let them know what your options are and try to make arrangements acceptable to them. You do not want your account to be marked as delinquent. Send some money in and let the creditor know when you will be able to make up the difference.

It is important that you use a calm, professional approach when dealing with your creditors. Explain your situation to them and then listen to what they have to say in response. Keep a mature attitude throughout the conversation. The last thing you can afford to do is irritate the creditor. By raising your voice and screaming like a raging lunatic you risk having the creditor refuse to work with you and possibly flagging your account as delinquent. STAY CALM . . . you are asking for a favor.

What To Do If Your Creditor Won't Work With You

When you experience a rare legitimate emergency, the likelihood of any creditor refusing to grant you a little leeway is slim. What happens if they do refuse to work with you? After all, you do have a signed agreement to pay a certain amount within a certain period of time, and the creditor does have the right to demand that the arrangement be honored.

If the creditor does refuse to allow you to make a late or partial payment, don't start screaming. Creditors hear excuses all the time and they have learned not to believe them. Try to reach a compromise in a calm fashion. If you cannot, just send in the full payment and go on to another creditor with your problem; maybe the next one will work with you. It would be quite unusual for all your creditors to deny you some leeway in the event of an emergency; in fact, the majority of them will work with you provided that the emergencies are few and far between.

If a creditor will work with you, you must abide by the new arrangements made during your crisis, whether it's allowing you to make smaller payments, skipping or stretching out payments, or reducing the interest rate for a period. However, don't ruin a good thing by forgetting or refusing to make up the late or missed payments once you're back on your feet. Remember, the creditor helped you when you needed help and you agreed to get caught up. Live up to the terms of the new, temporary arrangement or risk the situation backfiring.

Long Term Arrangements

The above example dealt with a one time cash flow problem. What happens if you lose your job or are laid up and can't work? Then what happens to your credit? In a case like this, make your full monthly payment and include a letter explaining your circumstances, then follow it up with a phone call. Let the creditor know how much you'll be able to send and steps you will take to get back on your regular payment schedule.

Many creditors will allow you to make smaller monthly payments provided they are made on time. YOU MUST ALWAYS SEND SOMETHING; as long as money comes in each month the creditor will probably keep the account open and active, and not put it in for collection. Send as much as you can afford. By continuing to pay during this down time you are showing them that you have every intention of fulfilling your obligations when you get back on your feet. Something is usually better than nothing.

Settlements

Another route you can take when you're strapped for money is to try to arrange a SETTLEMENT with a couple of your creditors, paying the bill off in full. Arrange as small a settlement as possible. It's a good idea to settle your total debt with as many creditors as possible when you lose your job or income. Borrow the money from any place you can. Many creditors would rather take less as payment in full than risk getting nothing at all.

Important "Don'ts"

DON'T wait for creditors to call you. Take the initiative and call them.

DON'T renege on new arrangements that have been made. Make your payments on time and for the required amount.

DON'T abuse the rare privilege of being allowed to pay a lesser amount. Your creditor isn't stupid and has heard the lies all too often. Ask for special arrangements only if the situation actually warrants it.

DON'T assume that it is okay to pay less than the required amount due. Only pay less if you have your creditor's authorization to do so.

DON'T ever scream or act abusively when dealing with a creditor.

DON'T ignore letters and payment requests.

DON'T forget to notify your creditors immediately if you change addresses.

As we've mentioned, your present creditors control your destiny; they rate your current payment history, and that will have the most influence on future creditors. Treat them fairly and with respect. By trying to take advantage of them, you only jeopordize your chances of obtaining additional credit by having them rate your account lower than the desired level.

5

Credit Bureaus and Credit Reports

We know that potential creditors request reports on your credit history when reviewing credit applications, but where do these reports come from? They come from CREDIT BUREAUS, which are warehouses of information on individuals and businesses. These bureaus gather, sort, and update the information, then relay it to creditors upon request. There are several hundred credit bureaus in the United States but only a few main ones. The big three are TRW, TRANS-UNION, and CBI (also known as EQUIFAX). Any time you apply for credit it's a good bet that one of these will convey your credit information to the institution of application.

The information comes from a variety of sources called AUTOMATIC SUBSCRIBERS. These subscribers include large banks, department stores, finance and mortgage companies, savings and loans, T&E card issuers, collection agencies, and many other types of creditors. These subscribers will report information on any individual or firm that does business with them, receiving, in return, discounts on credit reports they request.

Other information is gathered from public records such as bankruptcies, liens, judgments, garnishments, probations and other data from court records, county clerk offices and the bureaus own investigators.

Some creditors do not automatically report to credit bureaus. Some oil companies, insurance agencies, rental agents, medical facilities, utility companies, and some mortgage companies are among non-reporting companies. They will often, however, report if you renege on your contractual obligations or if they hire agencies to collect your debts or file legal actions against you.

All of the information, whether it's good or bad, is then either added to existing information or establishes a new report. Because of the tremendous amount of information available and the multiple agencies reporting and recording it, there may be errors in accuracy or completeness. The information may also differ from one bureau to the next. We will discuss ways to to correct these problems later in this chapter.

The Credit Report

All the information gathered at the credit bureaus are compiled into credit reports on people and, sometimes, businesses. Depending upon which bureau issues them, the reports may bear different information.

Two basic types of reports are issued by credit bureaus; these are the investigative and non-investigative reports. The latter is the most common.

The Investigative Report

This report details your credit history and your personal life. It is usually requested by employers on employees who are being considered for a major raise or important promotion that may require bonding or security clearance. Insurance companies often request this kind of report, although they usually utilize their own investigators.

The investigating agency will dispatch investigators to interview neighbors, friends, relatives and former employers (among others) in an attempt to discern your character and moral fiber. They will report anything they can which impacts your standards . . . whether or not you drink excessively, abuse your spouse or children, throw noisy parties, etc.

There usually is a limited amount of time to gather this information and, as a result, the report may contain erroneous information and hearsay. Your neighbor may be mad, and tell the investigator lies about you. These investigators are not as thorough as insurance or government investigators, and they may be criminally lax in following up on hearsay that could be highly detrimental to you. There are laws to protect you against fallacious investigative information.

An institution must notify you when they have requested an investigative report to be run. This requirement is detailed in The Fair Credit Reporting Act. The only exemptions to this law are government agencies and insurance companies using their own investigators, or when the investigation is being performed for an employer who is considering you for a position for which you did not apply. They neither have to notify you nor report the results of the investigation to you.

Immediately upon notification that an investigative report has been requested, you should send the agency a certified letter requesting a description of the investigation being conducted, the reason for it, the questions to be asked and of whom they will ask these questions. The agency has five (5) days to respond to your letter.

If the agency fails to respond within five days, send a second certified letter warning the agency that they are in violation of the law and that failure to respond to your request for the detailed information will result in a complaint being lodged against them with the Federal Trade Commission.

When you receive and review the response to your letter, you have the right to object to any of the proposed questions or to the entire investigation, demanding that it be stopped. You will, of course, risk the loss of the proposed promotion or position for which you've applied.

If you have no objections to what is proposed for the investigation, they may continue it. You then have the right to review the results of the investigation, free of charge, regardless of whether it is favorable or detrimental to you and your credit file. They do not have to show you the actual report nor do they have to release the names of the persons who gave information on you, and medical information divulged does not have to be released in specifics. You must, however, be informed of the reports contents.

The Non-Investigative Report

This is the most common report issued by credit bureaus, and contains only information that is provided by subscribers to the bureau. Obviously, the more credit you have established, the more information will appear on your credit report. Even if you have no credit there may still be items on your report, such as inquiries by other potential creditors, accounts placed with collection agencies, or judgments obtained against you (perhaps for non-payment of rent or medical bills). Regardless of whether or not you have any prior credit established, when you renege on a payment plan or rental agreement you risk having negative comments included on your report.

Although these reports differ in appearance from one bureau to the next, they all contain five basic sections (see page 42). These sections are: Personal Information, History or Tradelines, Inquiries, Public Records and Consumer Statement. We will now discuss each section in detail so you will have an idea of how to read your report.

Personal Information

Charles C. Consumer	SSN: 123-45-6789
CA: 1221 Main St.	CE: Smiths Auto Body
Anytown, Il. 60025	Anytown, Il.
FA: 1234 Elm St.	FE: Jacksons Garage
Thistown, Wi. 52001	Thattown, Wi.

Tradelines

CREDITOR	RPT Date	OPEN Date	HIGH Credit	CURR Bal	PAST Due	MOS Rev	30	60	90
B ABC Mortgage								M-1	
12345	08/93	02/90	100000	95000	12	0 0 0	360x800		
B GMAC								I-1	
2312	08/93	04/92	13000	12250	16	0 0 0	48x225		

Inquiries: 08/12/93 MBNA
                      08/22/93 FIRST CARD

Public Records: NONE

Consumer Statement: NONE

The Five Main Sections of the Credit Report

The PERSONAL INFORMATION section contains your name, social security number, present and previous addresses, employment information, etc. The bureau will try to obtain as much information as possible for this section with the intent of more properly matching new information to existing information or preventing consumers from changing information solely to hide previously recorded bad debts.

The next section is the history section, also known as the TRADELINES. This section lists all of the credit you have established (provided the creditor is a subscriber), status of the account (paid, current, closed, etc), type of account (individual or joint), credit limit, balance, payment history and when the account was opened. Collection accounts may also appear as a tradeline.

Refer to the figure on Page 42. The tradelines are read as follows: Account Designations (B=borrower; C=co-borrower; J=joint; U=undesignated)-Creditor Name (who extended the credit)-Type of Account (O=open account, where payment is due in full each month or as agreed with creditor; R=revolving, where minimum payments are due, such as with some charge cards; I=installment, such as for car and other loans; M=mortgage; C=credit line)-Rating (given by the creditor, 0=new account too early to rate, 1=pays as agrees, 2=usually not more than one payment past due, 3=usually 2 payments past due or pays more than 60 days late, 4=usually 3 or more payments past due or pays more than 90 days late, 5=120 days or more past due, 7=account in wage earner plan or Chapter 13 bankruptcy, 8=merchandise repossessed or fore-closure, 9=bad debt collection, charge off, judgment, suit, skip, Chapter 7 bankruptcy, UR= unrated)-Account Number (this number may be scrambled or incomplete on the report to protect the consumer)-Reporting Date (last date creditor reported to the bureau)-Open Date (date account was opened)-High Credit (credit limit or amount of loan)-Current Balance-Past Due (amount past due)-Months Reviewed (number of months creditor reviewed to rate your account)-30, 60, 90 (late days, if payments were 30, 60, or 90 days late the number of times they were that late will be listed here)-Payments or Length of Contract (360x250 means $250 for 360 months, 10 mos means 10 months to pay).

The third section of the report lists the INQUIRIES. These are the various agencies that, for whatever reason, request a copy of your credit report. They could be potential creditors judging you for credit-worthiness, current creditors wishing to raise your current limit, third parties such as collection agencies, or banks where you are opening a checking or savings account. Inquiries generally stay on your report for 90 days.

Tax liens, judgments, bankruptcies and collection agency referrals are covered in the next section, known as PUBLIC RECORDS. This information is always negative, so you should always avoid having anything appear in this section. Other things that may show up here, although not very often, are imprisonments and probations, foreclosures, and divorces.

The final section is one that few people know exists but may very well be the most important one on the report. This section allows you, as the consumer, to tell your side of the story. It's called the CONSUMER STATEMENT and enables you to clarify any

item on the report that you feel needs to be explained. You can place into your record statements
that you believe will have mitigating impact on possibly negative appearing items on your report, such as
late payments, collections, or charge-offs. We have
reviewed thousands of credit reports and have seen
only a handful of consumer statements listed. You
can and should use this section to your benefit because, many times, a creditor may overlook something that you've taken the time to explain. The statement cannot exceed 100 words in length.

Reviewing and Correcting Your Report

According to the Equal Credit Opportunity Act, any
institution denying you credit must furnish, in writing,
their reasons for the credit refusal. They must also
include the name, address and phone number of any
credit bureau from whom they requested your credit
report. The telephone number given for the bureau
will probably play a recorded message telling you
how to go about getting a copy of your credit report.
Write the bureau within thirty days of your denial and
request a copy of your report. It must be provided
free of charge as long as it is requested within 30 days
of being denied credit. You may also call and make
an appointment to review the report in person with a
representative available to answer any questions you
may have (don't allow the representative to rush
through the report; you have the right to know what it
says). If you haven't been denied credit but still want
a copy of your report, and we recommend getting a
copy of your report at least once a year, contact the

credit bureaus at the addresses listed at the end of this chapter. You may be charged a nominal fee which you should include with your written request.

Here's the specific procedure to follow: Make a copy of the credit denial letter and send it, certified mail, along with your written request, to the credit bureau. Your letter must include any information the bureau requested to speed up the return. You should receive your report within 2 to 4 weeks. You will not receive your actual credit report, but you must be provided with the following: The "nature and substance" of all information the report contains on you, sources of this information and a list of all inquiries made within at least the last 6 months. Many bureaus will also include a brochure explaining the consumer statement (which we've already covered) and how to read and dispute items on the report (which we will cover next).

When you receive your report review it carefully. If you don't know the meaning of a certain item, look it up or ask someone who may be knowledgeable on credit reports. Check the inquiries first. Assure yourself that they were all made by creditors to whom you've applied for credit. If you're uncertain about why one or more appear on the report ask the bureau for the name and address of them and why the inquiry was done. It may turn out to be an outside collection agency representing one of your creditors, or a financial institution financing a purchase from a store or car dealer.

It is unlawful for a creditor from whom you did not request credit or any agency who is not representing a current creditor to do an inquiry on your report, although companies considering you for pre-approved applications or to increase your current line of credit may pull a copy of your report. If an inquiry is unauthorized, write a letter to the inquiring agency informing them that they are in violation of the FAIR CREDIT REPORTING ACT. Strongly suggest that they remove the inquiry or face the filing of a complaint with the Federal Trade Commission.

Once you've reviewed and corrected the inquiry section to your satisfaction, go to the credit history section. This is the most difficult section to decipher. Because credit bureaus key in on names first, the first thing you should do is make sure all of the credit listed is yours. Credit reports will often contain information on others who may have a name similar to yours. Once you're certain all the credit is yours, look for negative information (accounts closed by creditors, repossessions, foreclosures, write-offs due to bad payment histories, collection accounts) and note the age of the information. If the information is recent you may want to send a consumer statement explaining why the accounts are listed negatively.

If the information is inaccurate, you can shift the burden of proof on its accuracy to the very creditors that listed it on your report. This is precisely what credit counselors and those "improve your credit" ads do. Why not do it yourself and save the money? This can be done in two different ways. You can send a certified letter along with a copy of the credit report, with disputed items highlighted, to the bureau stating that you disagree with the entry on your report and that you consider it detrimental to your total credit history. The bureau has "a reasonable amount of time" (30 days maximum) to investigate your claim; they contact the specific creditor for verification of the negative remark.

The other way to dispute the items is to contact the creditors yourself and have them send letters to the bureau requesting the adverse data to be removed. We prefer this method for 2 reasons: first, many creditors would much rather deal with you, their customer, than a third party such as the credit bureau, so your chances of satisfaction are greater; and second, they can send you a copy of the letter they will send to the bureau so you will have a backup should the credit bureau not honor the initial request. This second approach is especially good if you are dealing with late payments that you feel are errors, although some creditors prefer to work only with the credit bureaus.

Regardless of which method you use, if you're contesting an older account chances are the creditor will no longer have the information necessary to verify its accuracy. By law, the item must then be removed from your report. Frequently, a creditor just won't take the time to respond to the request for verification and, again, the item must then be removed. If the creditor does furnish proof that the item is correct, you may want to write a consumer statement explaining your side of the story.

IT'S EASY FOR CREDITORS TO HAVE ENTRIES LISTED ON A CREDIT REPORT. MANY CREDITORS WILL NOT UPDATE NOR REMOVE DATED INFORMATION ON THEIR OWN. YOU MUST TAKE THE INITIATIVE BY REVIEWING THE MATERIAL AND EITHER REQUEST INVESTIGATIONS FROM THE CREDIT BUREAU OR CONTACT THE CREDITORS CONCERNING REMOVAL OF THE DISPUTED ITEMS. CONCENTRATE ON AREAS THAT WILL BE MOST DETRIMENTAL TO YOUR ABILITY TO RECEIVE CREDIT. BY FOLLOWING THESE PROCEDURES IT IS

POSSIBLE TO TOTALLY REWRITE YOUR REPORT, IN YOUR FAVOR, WITHIN A COUPLE MONTHS TIME.

If your history section isn't in need of correction, leave it alone. Go on to the public record section. This section lists bankruptcies, tax liens, judgments, and sometimes collection accounts. It may also contain divorce or arrest information, but very seldom. This is the most deleterious data on your report. You can write a consumer statement explaining the factors that led to the placement of adverse data in this section, but YOU CANNOT GET THESE STATEMENTS REMOVED PRIOR TO THE DATES SET BY LAW, UNLESS AGREED TO BY ALL PARTIES INVOLVED, THE ITEMS ARE ERRONEOUS, OR IF AN INVESTIGATION FAILS TO VERIFY THE DATA. YOU CAN CHANGE THE STATUS OF THE ENTRIES BY PAYING OFF LIENS, JUDGMENTS OR COLLECTION ACCOUNTS (see the section on Obsolete Information for length of time the items may remain on your report).

Be aware that if the disputed item appears on more than one bureau, it may be necessary to repeat the steps and file separate disputes for each bureau. In June of 1994 a system was to be in place that would allow consumers to file a dispute once and have it passed on to all bureaus involved, but this has not proven to be the case. Play it safe and send your disputes to each bureau separately, and remember to send all correspondence certified mail.

Adding Favorable Information

It is possible to add favorable information to your credit report even though there is no law on the books that grants you this right. The Fair Credit Reporting Act does state, however, that credit bureaus should allow you to add information to your report when the absence of any information could lead to the denial of requested credit. The bureau has the right to charge a small fee for this service.

The type of information that is most beneficial to add includes repaid debts that haven't appeared on the report, utilities, and rent payments. Send a certified letter to the bureau asking that they contact the creditor and ask for the okay to list the account. Be certain that any of this information is verifiable . . . the bureau will investigate its accuracy.

Your New and Improved Credit

You've put in the time and effort to straighten up your credit, so now you need to know what to do with it. Send a certified letter to the credit bureau stating that you want copies of your new report sent to all creditors who have done an inquiry within the past 6 months, to any potential employer who inquired within the past two years, and to you. You must DEMAND that the bureau do this; they won't send revised reports voluntarily.

Follow up on your demands to assure yourself that the bureau has complied with them. You can request a copy of your updated report from the bureau or reapply to creditors that turned you down based on your old credit report. If they still deny you credit, the bureau may not have supplied them with an updated credit report. Contact the bureau and demand it be sent.

IT'S A GOOD IDEA TO REQUEST A COPY OF YOUR CREDIT REPORT ONCE A YEAR TO MAKE CERTAIN IT REMAINS ACCURATE AND UPDATED ACCORDINGLY. The low fee will be a wise investment.

Obsolete or Adverse Information

The Fair Credit Reporting Act tells us that there is information that can only remain on a credit report for a certain length of time. Once the specified period of time has elapsed, by law that information must be removed by the bureaus. Although they are not required to do so, the bureaus can keep that removed information in a separate file. The lengths of time for keeping various data may change from state to state; check the law in your state for particulars. The following are Federal guidelines on maximum allowable time for keeping data on your credit report:

DATA		KEPT NO LONGER THAN
Chapter 7 Bankruptcy	*	10 years
Chapter 13 Bankruptcy	*	7 years
Suits & Judgments	*	7 years or till expiration of Governing statute.
Tax Liens	*	7 years
Collection Accounts	*	7 years from charge off date
Write-offs	*	7 years
Arrests & convictions	*	7 years
Other adverse information	*	7 years

The above mentioned items cannot, by themselves, be used to deny you credit, but when they are combined with other criteria, they may result in creditors refusing to grant you credit. It is important that you know the laws as they are written in your state, and that a reporting agency strictly abide by those laws.

There are, however, exceptions to the law. When a credit transaction involves $50,000 or more, if one is applying for life insurance valued at $50,000 or more, or when an employer requests a report on an employee applying for a position salaried at $20,000 or more, the bureau may report on negative information long after it has been removed from the report. For this reason, it is a good idea to persuade the bureau not to keep a separate file of adverse information.

Check with your local library or contact the Federal Trade Commission if you wish further information on the Fair Credit Reporting Act.

Complaints

Whenever you request action from a credit bureau, keep a copy of all correspondence for your records. Send every letter certified mail. Follow up on your requests to see that they're being honored. If they are not you will have copies of the correspondence that you can use to file complaints with the FTC.

If the initial request was not honored send a second letter, certified mail, warning them that they are in violation of the law and risk further action by not honoring your request. Usually, the implied threat in the second letter will spur them to action. If your second letter is ignored, you should file a complaint with the FTC. Please note that the FTC will act only on complaints that affect the general public, so word your complaint to make it clear that others persons can be and are negatively affected by the bureaus reticence to respond to your request. You have many rights under the Fair Credit Reporting Act, including the right to sue creditors and bureaus alike for noncompliance, and must use them to your benefit.

The Credit Revolution

Your credit history is yours for life, and for that reason it should be as accurate as possible. As we have stated, creditors are quick to add something to a credit report but very lax in showing accounts paid, closed, or transferred. Although laws are in place to protect the consumer against such misinformation on their credit report, and some credit bureaus and creditors are offering specialized service and using more sophisticated means to minimize errors, when they are cited for violations, the punishment is less than severe and little is done to see that the mistakes are not repeated.

The Fair Credit Reporting Act was written in 1970 and has never been amended. In 1994, both the House and Senate passed individual bills in hopes of improving the FCRA. Unfortunately, Congress adjourned without an agreement being reached, so consumers still need to get involved. The credit bureaus deny that a problem exists, so if consumers don't come forward and let Congress know about the severity of the problem, they can only rely on what the lobbyists are telling them. WE, AS CONSUMERS,

MUST BECOME INVOLVED!!! A CREDIT REVOLU-
TION IS WHAT IS NEEDED TO PROVOKE THESE
PEOPLE TO ACTION!!!

Have you ever seen any of the following on your
credit report?:

Tradelines, inquiries, collection accounts, liens,
judgments, or bankruptcies that aren't yours?

Accounts that have been transferred or paid but
are not showing a zero balance?

Information that remains erroneously reported after
the creditor has told the bureau to delete or correct it?

Data that is more than 7 years old by last reporting
date?

Different bureaus showing different payment history?

Collection accounts that were paid long ago not
being shown as paid?

Creditors or inquiries that you were not familiar
with and had no phone number so you could contact
them?

Bankruptcies, judgments, or liens that you know
have been satisfied but are not being reflected as
such?

Major lenders such as mortgage companies not
reporting your payment history?

Information that just hasn't been updated?

Accounts that were discharged in a bankruptcy
but are still being reported as collections or charge
offs?

Mistakes that were previously removed showing
up again later?

Are you frustrated by the fact that, in many cases,
you get a problem cleared with one bureau only to be
told you need to repeat the entire process to get it
cleared up with a second bureau?

If you can answer Yes to any of the above questions (and we'll bet close to half of you will), it is something that needs to be addressed. The bureaus should make it accessible to consumers to contact unfamiliar creditors, and should act promptly when a creditor requests that information be corrected, but they often don't. They should be responsible for reporting updated and accurate information on collection accounts, charge-offs, bankruptcies, judgments, and liens, but they aren't. The bureaus are not entirely to blame, however. The creditors should act responsibly and provide the necessary information in a timely manner, especially in the case of adverse credit. We have had access to thousands of credit reports and are appalled at the lackadaisical approach that the bureaus (and in some cases creditors) take toward YOUR credit. Who is effected by this attitude? YOU ARE!!!

The amendments that were passed in 1994 consisted of changesin the prices charged to consumers for copies of their credit report, easier access to the bureaus, more stringent policy on length of time they have to correct errors, and making creditors responsible for accuracy. Although this is a start, it is by no means enough. The system should be made more cost efficient to encourage creditors to report accurate information. Penalties for noncompliance should be strict and consistant for creditors and bureaus alike. Bureaus should furnish consumers with phone numbers for creditors appearing on their credit reports and improve the dispute/investigation procedure so it only needs to be done once to cover all 3 bureaus.

Anyone who has ever attempted to correct a problem on their report knows how frustrating it can be to get things accomplished as the system now stands. Changes have to be made to make it easier and less time consuming for the consumer, so it's important that consumers get involved in this legislative process. If you haven't requested a copy of your credit report lately, get one, especially if you are going to be applying for a large loan such as a mortgage. If there are no problems on your report, you are indeed fortunate. If there are problems, now is the time to correct them. Don't rely on someone to do it for you; take the initiative and do it yourself, and while your at it, write a letter to your Congressperson explaining the problems you encountered on your report. Tell him/her you'd like to see changes made and offer your suggestions. If enough people join the credit revolution, maybe we can get some laws changed to make it easier for us. We recommend that all interested parties continue to monitor the various media outlets for information pertaining to the credit bureaus. After all, the Fair Credit Reporting Act was written for the benefit of the consumer, so why is the consumer the one paying the price? (See Chapter 12 for more information).

The Credit Bureau Addresses

As we have stated at the beginning of this chapter, TransUnion, TRW, and Equifax are the 3 major credit reporting companies. All other credit reporting agencies will get their information from one or more of these, so accusing a smaller agency of putting erroneous information on your credit report or asking them to remove erroneous information from your permanent file is futile; it must be done through the major credit bureaus.

The addresses and phone numbers for the Big 3 are:

TRW	Equifax
P.O. Box 2350	P.O. Box 740241
Chatsworth, CA. 91313	Atlanta, GA. 30374
800/682-7654	800/685-1111

TransUnion Corp.
Customer Relations Dept.
P.O. Box 7000 Dept. P
North Olmsted, OH   44070
800/851-2674

Remember that if you've been denied credit within 30 days of writing, include a copy of your denial letter and you will receive a free report, otherwise there may be a minimal charge.

TRW is currently offering a free report to anyone who requests one. Write to the above address, and be sure to include the following information any time you request a copy of your credit report:

Full Name including Jr. or Sr.

Current Address

Former Address for previous 5 years

Phone Number

Birthday

Social Security Number

Spouses Name if it applies.

Photocopy of drivers license or social security
    card

If additional information is required, the credit bureau will contact you.

6

Women and Credit

Not very long ago it was common practice among creditors to deny credit to women, even though they may have had their own source of income and the willingness and ability to pay their own bills. The reason stems from the erroneous idea that all women would eventually marry, have children and then rely on their spouse's income for support.

As more and more complaints were lodged about credit denial for reasons of sex and marital status, the decision was made to study the situation and determine the accuracy and basis of the complaints.

In 1972 the National Commission on Consumer Finance reached the following conclusions:

1) Single women had a harder time establishing credit than single men regardless of similarities in financial history and ability;

2) Married women were required to apply for credit under their husband's name;

3) A married woman's income was not considered on joint credit applications; and

4) Widowed and divorced women had an unreasonably difficult time in obtaining credit.

These conclusions lead to the writing of the EQUAL CREDIT OPPORTUNITY ACT (ECOA), which made it unlawful to deny credit based on sex and marital status. The Act later was amended to include race, color, national origin, religion, age and the receipt of public assistance.

This is not a chapter on the ECOA, although this law is quite important. This chapter was written to inform women of their credit rights. Knowing ones rights always assists in minimizing discrimination.

Federal Rights for Women

Prior to the enactment of the law, creditors would deny credit to women based upon sexual connotations ascribed to job titles. Women who listed their jobs as waitress on credit applications were denied while men listing jobs as waiter were approved for credit more frequently. This practice has been minimized but still exists. Check the reasons for denial of your credit applications and determine if they were based upon discrimination.

Women CANNNOT be denied credit based upon their marital status. Creditors CANNOT question women about their future plans for marriage or divorce. The only permissible question relates to the number of dependents a woman has and the cost of raising them.

Married women can apply for credit using their married or maiden name, or both. If credit has been established using your maiden name you need not reapply using your married name. The opposite applies as well. Women once married and now widowed, divorced or separated need not reapply under their new status, unless the credit was derived by using your mates income and credit history. Then you would possibly have to reapply, but only if your own income, at the time, was not sufficient to maintain the credit.

A creditor cannot require a woman to obtain a cosigner unless the credit application is a joint one. If the application is for you alone and your income is sufficient to warrant the approval based upon the creditors criteria, you do not need a cosigner unless the same requirement is levied upon males.

The only time a creditor can ask a woman questions about her marital status or husband is when her spouse would be allowed use of the credit line or account, or if she is relying on money supplied from her spouse to maintain an adequate income for credit. If your income and credit history are solid enough to be extended credit on your own, your spouse's occupation is immaterial to any credit application.

A divorced or separated woman does not need to list alimony on applications UNLESS it is necessary to meet repayment obligations.

You cannot be denied credit simply by indicating you are employed part time, although a creditor may inquire as to the duration and reliability of income derived from such employment. Remember that the title of housewife is an unsalaried title and not applicable to use on individual credit applications, although it may be used on joint applications.

Comments made by prospective creditors that are discouraging are considered unlawful. Some examples of sexist remarks used simply to discourage women from applying for credit are: "Women with children are seldom extended credit" or "Your husband should apply with you."

If you feel you've been the victim of credit discrimination, talk to an attorney or possibly a women's rights organization and get assistance in pursuing a redress to the discrimination.

State Laws

Many states have enacted laws against discrimination that may be more stringent than the Federal laws. Check with your local library or Attorney General's office for more information.

If you are ready to pursue a case of discrimination, you will have to decide whether to file a State or Federal complaint; you cannot file both. Consult with your attorney.

Who is Covered by the ECOA

The following types of companies MUST ALWAYS ABIDE BY THE ECOA:

Banks, savings and loans, mortgage lenders, credit card issuers, sales finance companies (appliances, automobiles, etc.), loan companies and consumer leasing companies.

The remaining companies are covered by the ECOA but are granted special exemptions by the government:

Utility companies, credit arrangers (car dealers, real estate brokers), companies that extend credit for business, commercial or agricultural purposes, incidental creditors (doctors, dentists), and certain state and federal agencies (FHA, Small Business Administration, Veterans Administration).

Married Women and Credit

A single woman should no longer have trouble establishing credit as long as she is credit worthy. A married woman should concentrate on establishing credit in her own name. If her credit was establish before she married it should be kept in her maiden name, although she may still apply for credit jointly with her spouse. Women who have never established credit before marrying should concentrate on establishing it now that they are married. By preparing for the unexpected one can avoid possible difficulties in the future. Should a marriage collapse, a woman without established credit will find herself in a serious problematic situation.

How to Establish Your Own Credit

The first thing you must do is open a savings account in your own name, either maiden name or married name. If you're working, deposit a portion of each paycheck into the account. If you are not employed, borrow some money from family or friends (including your husband) to establish the savings account.

Once the account is open, talk to the bank personnel about obtaining a secured loan or bank card, explaining that you are in the process of establishing your own credit. Tell them that you will use your savings account as collateral. If you're a good customer, the bank may allow your request even if what you ask is not within their normal policy guidelines. If they refuse your request, apply for a loan at a finance company or for a charge card through a department store or lending institution.

When you receive your credit make your payments on time. If you get a loan you may want to put the loan money in a savings account so that it will draw interest while you are repaying it. If you get a bank card, use it sparingly. Following several months of careful budgeting you'll be able to apply for additional credit. Now you're on your way to establishing your own solid credit history. You may want to request a copy of your credit report to ascertain whether or not your accounts are being reported to the credit bureau.

A married woman's credit history is often nonexistent because credit is often reported as the spouse's. If you have an account, the payment history should be reflected under your name. Check your report and notify the bureau and your creditors as to how to report on your accounts. If you and your spouse use the account jointly, have the history reported as such.

Why a Married Woman
Should Have Her Own Credit

Marriages frequently end in divorce; when they do, credit becomes a very real problem for a woman. If all the credit was established in your spouse's name or in both of your names, you'll have nothing to use when he's out the door. Remove your name from all joint accounts by getting a copy of your credit report and contacting the creditors. If you are a secondary user or cosigner, your spouse may have to contact the creditor and have your name removed. Either way, in the event of divorce, seperate yourself from your spouse and get credit in your own name. Don't rely on a marital settlement agreement as a means to get your name cleared of obligations you might have jointly with your husband. MARITAL SETTLEMENT AGREEMENTS are contracts, determined by the court, that determine who will be responsible for the payment of what bills in the event of divorce. THEY ARE NOT BINDING IN THE EYES OF YOUR CREDITORS! INSTALLMENT LOANS WILL NEED TO BE RENEGO-TIATED OR REFINANCED IN THE NAME OF THE PERSON WHO WILL BE RESPONSIBLE FOR MAKING THE PAYMENTS. CLOSE AS MANY ACCOUNTS AS POSSIBLE AND ESTABLISH NEW CREDIT IN YOUR OWN NAME. If you already have your own credit, your spouses departure will be much less of a financial shock.

Even if the marriage survives, having credit established in your own name will give you a means of support should your spouse lose his job, permanently or temporarily. With good credit, you could apply for a loan in your name and continue to meet the obligations the two of you have.

Many companies will transfer accounts originally placed in your spouse's name to your name in the event of his death. The company may, however, request that you reapply for the credit . . . especially if the original account was obtained listing only your deceased husband's sources of income. Even if all his accounts remain open after his death, without having established yourself as credit worthy you won't be able to obtain additional and different credit.

These are several of the most obvious reasons why it's important for you to establish your own credit. There are many other reasons, several of them highly immoral. With your own credit, you can maintain your self image in the face of any adversity.

Marital Status Discrimination and the Law

Many creditors still wrongly assume that with married couples the male controls the finances. They will periodically ask a woman (in either a delicate or indelicate manner) if her husband knows she is applying for credit. If you are credit worthy, it's no ones business but your own. If you are applying for an unsecured account in your name, the creditor may not inquire about your marital status, unless you reside in a COMMUNITY PROPERTY state (where ownership is equal between you and your spouse) and property is being used as a means of collateral. Even in this type of situation only the terms married, unmarried or separated can be used.

In community property states, if you qualify for credit and wish to place household property as collateral against loans, you don't need your spouse to cosign; you control 50% of the property. The creditor may question you about your spouse in an attempt to determine if the possibility exists that both partners may be using the same property as collateral against different obligations. The legal status of this question has not been determined and, as a result, both partners may be required to affix their signatures to certain credit applications.

Married women sometimes are given joint accounts when they apply for separate ones. The reason given by creditors is that state law prohibits a married woman from obtaining individual credit lines. The ECOA allows state laws to be preempted provided the creditor receives the woman's promise that she is personally responsible for repayment.

If you are being denied credit because of your husband's bad credit history, contact potential creditors and offer proof that the credit history they are basing your denials on does not reflect your credit worthiness, but your spouse's fouled credit.

If the creditor requires you to have a cosigner, they cannot demand that the cosigner be your husband. He may cosign if he is willing, but any qualified person may cosign.

In the event of a change of marital status, the creditor may not require you to reapply, change the terms of the contract, or terminate the contract unless it can be proved that there is evidence of unwillingness or inability to pay, although it is to your benefit to close or remove your name from as many joint accounts as possible in the event of divorce.

More information on the specific laws pertaining to marital status and credit can be obtained through women's groups and the state and federal government.

Discrimination Complaints

What can you do if you feel you've been a victim of credit discrimination? Contact the creditor and request a meeting to discuss the denial. The creditor may be unaware of the violation perpetrated. Tell the creditor what specific law has been violated under the ECOA. Merely the mention of specific violations may be sufficient to get the creditor to revise his consideration of your application. The creditor may consult the company legal department for verification of your complaint before reconsidering your application, but it will be reconsidered.

If this initial meeting is unsuccessful in turning the creditor around, prepare a letter specifying your complaint and send it to the company president. You can identify who the president is with a simple phone call to the company. Note that if the violation is not corrected immediately, legal action may be necessary. Always specify the violations. Send the letter certified mail, specify a deadline for a response, and keep a copy of the letter for your files.

If the complaint letter still does not stir the creditor to action, you should then go to the Federal Government. To identify which agency handles your particular complaint send a letter to the Division of Consumer Affairs, Federal Reserve Board, Washington, D.C. They will forward your letter to the appropriate agency or notify you as to where you can send your complaint. In the letter, explain the situation, the action you've taken, and include copies of correspondence between you and the creditor in question (remember to log dates, times, and names). The agency is not required by law to respond to your complaint; they may contact the creditor and urge reconsideration of the application, as well as a change in any questionable practices.

Either the creditor will then contact you with their decision or the government agency will contact you with the results of their investigation (if there was one) and what legal rights you have. They may also turn your complaint over to the United States Attorney General if your complaint is identical to many others received through their offices.

You now need to make a decision on whether or not to sue the discriminating creditor. Reassess your situation, making certain that your complaint is stronger than any defense the creditor may present (your possible bad credit worthiness). If you decide your case is strong, retain an attorney for a legal opinion.

Decide if the potential time and cost of suing is worth your effort. You have up to two years to file suit.

Additional information may be obtained by reviewing the Equal Credit Opportunity Act. This law was written primarily to address the discrimination rampant against women. It can, however, in certain instances, be applicable to situations of discrimination against males. Know the law and use it to protect and enrich your life.

Medical Bills and Credit

The only time medical bills will appear on your credit report is when they go unpaid. Otherwise exemplary reports are frequently tarnished by the inclusion of unpaid medical and dental bills. The entries, although negative, may be overlooked by creditors as late insurance payments, but they will still have negative impact on future credit approval. Previously, few hospitals and clinics reported to credit bureaus; many more are reporting now due to the increased number of unpaid bills.

Medical bills are not usually planned expenses. They may be among the largest bills incurred by a family and people may assume that since they were incurred through no fault of their own, the bills needn't be retired as quickly as other, discretionary bills. THEY NEED TO BE PAID. Unlike other creditors, hospitals and doctors can't refuse to treat emergency situations nor can they discharge ill patients before it is safe to do so. They will, however, take action against persons who refuse to settle their bills. There are a number of ways to avoid having unpaid medical bills tarnish otherwise good credit reports, although it may require initiative on your part to get them paid.

Insurance Companies

With the cost of health care steadily rising, health insurance is now more of a necessity than ever in handling unexpected, large medical bills. With such importance placed in this insurance, it is necessary to be intimately knowledgeable of its specific coverages and requirements.

First and foremost, you should know what your policy states. You must know the percentage of the bills your insurance covers, the deductible that's your responsibility, what items or procedures are not covered and whether pre-authorization is required prior to hospital admittance. Many HMO's have specific requirements that, if not followed, void your insurance coverage.

When you read your policy take notes of the portions you do not understand and ask your agent or personnel department to explain them to you. Knowing the specifics of what your insurance does and does not cover will save you time and money, and help you avoid potentially serious problems. Once you know your coverage, you will be better equipped to deal with your medical bills.

The Insurance Claim

Once you've followed any rules concerning pre-notification to or pre-authorization from your insurance company, you're ready for your hospital or doctor visit. Whether it's for a routine checkup or major surgery, you will probably need to have an insurance claim form completed. Some insurance companies don't require one; find out before your visit. If you do need one, get it from your employer or insurance company before your visit and bring it with you.

The claim form has different sections; you will have to complete your section and sign it. There are two others sections that are optional but should also be signed. The first is the assignment of benefits section, which allows the insurance company to pay directly to the provider of services, and the second is for the release of additional information, which the insurance company often requests. The other sections are for information to be provided by the hospital or doctor and may not necessarily need to be completed. When you visit the provider ask if they will file the insurance claim for you. If they will, give them a copy of your insurance card and the claim form so they can submit the bill to the insurance company for processing. If the provider won't bill the insurance, and there are some that won't, ask for an itemized bill so you can submit it to your insurance carrier with the claim form. YOU MUST HAVE AN ITEMIZED BILL (preferably one called a UB-92); NO INSURANCE COMPANY WILL PAY WITHOUT ONE. If you don't get one upon leaving the provider, get a firm commitment to have them send it as soon as possible, and always keep a copy for your records.

If you do have to file your own insurance claim, you may not have to have the provider fill out his part of the form, provided you can get a bill that has all the pertinent information the insurance company needs to process the claim. Many insurance payments are delayed because the provider doesn't have the time to fill out the claim form immediately. Most insurance companies will accept an incomplete claim form, provided the following information is included on the bill: Provider name, provider number, doctor name (if different from provider name), patient name, diagnosis, description of services received, date of service and charges for each procedure.

All of this information can be obtained on what's called a UB-92. If you can get a copy of this bill, submit it; if you can't, submit the regular itemized bill and the insurance company will notify you or the provider if additional information is needed.

Following Up On Your Claim

Follow up on your insurance claim can be time consuming, but it is an important and necessary step in making certain your bill gets paid promptly. By staying on top of your claim, you will know what is happening with it and what, if anything, is needed to process it. Many people just sit back and wait once the claim is filed, then are shocked when after 4 or 5 months the bill still hasn't been paid. By staying in contact with the insurance company as well as the provider, things will get done a lot more quickly.

If the provider was going to submit the claim to your insurance company, check with them a after a week or so and make sure it has been done. They will usually send you a statement that will say the insurance was billed. If it wasn't billed, find out why; maybe they didn't have the correct billing address. Some insurance companies require the claim to go through the insured's place of employment, so be sure to tell the provider if this is the case. Improper billing will only delay the payment.

If the claim was filed, allow another week and check with your insurance company, or place of employment if the claim was sent there. If it went through your job, make sure they sent it to the insurance company promptly. You may want to ask your insurance representative at work to do the follow up for you, although it's better to do it yourself. The important thing here is to make sure that the insurance company receives the bill before too much time has elapsed.

When you call the insurance company, you will need to know the information on your insurance card, the date of service, and the original amount of the bill. With this information, they will be able to tell you whether or not they received the claim. If they haven't received it, ask how long it takes for the claim to show up on their system and call back after that time has elapsed.

Don't assume that just because the provider filed the claim they will follow up on it, because they won't. They deal with many claims every day and cannot properly follow up on all of them. You, on the other hand, only have to be concerned with one claim, so it would be to your benefit to do your own follow up.

If Your Claim Wasn't Received

If, after an appropriate length of time, the insurance company still doesn't have your claim, get the mailing address and the name of a person to whom you can send the bill. By sending the claim to no one in particular, any number of people might handle the claim before it gets to the proper party. All this handling takes valuable time; try to find out who handles your claim and send it directly to that person.

Contact the provider and inform them that the claim was never received by the insurance company. Ask them either to rebill the insurance, which they may not do immediately, or to send you the bill so you can submit it yourself (if you followed our advice and kept a copy for your files, you won't need to ask for another). Since you will probably need another claim form, it would be better for you to rebill the insurance yourself. You may have to call them more than once, but don't waste valuable time. The longer it takes the insurance company to receive the claim, the longer the bill goes unpaid, and the more likely it is that the account will be placed in collections.

Send the new bill and claim form, and follow up with the person you previously spoke to and make sure the claim was received.

When Your Claim Has Been Received

When you get verification that the claim was received by the insurance company, ask if any additional information is needed. Many times, especially if the hospital visit was due to an accident, the insurance company will need details. If they ask for them, send them immediately. They may also request information about another insurance carrier you might have. Again, send the requested information; don't waste time, or you may forget and the bill will never get paid.

The insurance company might need hospital records. They will probably request them from the provider, but you may have to sign a release form at the hospital before the records are sent.

Contact the provider and find out their policy for releasing information, and if you must sign a release form, do it immediately. Then follow up and make sure the records are sent to the insurance company. If not, call the provider again; by staying on top of the situation you'll get things accomplished.

When the insurance company has everything they need to process the claim, ask them how long it will take to be paid. If they don't give you a definite date, ask when it would be okay to call back, then make sure you do. Stay on their back if that's what it takes to get the bill paid. Many insurance companies are notoriously slow payers, so sometimes the only way to get things done is to make a nuisance of yourself.

Now it's your turn to request something. Once everything is in order, the claim has been processed and, hopefully, paid, have the insurance company send you an EXPLANATION OF BENEFITS (EOB). The EOB lists the amount of the bill paid and what portion was denied. The amount they paid will be reflected in the percentage statement on the EOB; you will also have a statement of how much of your deductible was met. The EOB will be your record of what you've paid toward your deductible, so even if you know the bill will be applied to your deductible, submit it anyhow. In the event the claim was denied, the EOB will also list the reason for denial.

Lastly, if you failed to authorize the assignment of benefits, the insurance company will send the claim payment directly to you. You will then be required to pay the provider. NEVER USE THE INSURANCE CHECK ON ANYTHING OTHER THAN PAYING THE PROVIDER'S BILL. Should you be tempted, realize that the provider will show no mercy in their collection efforts when they find out. You will also face the possibility of being charged with insurance fraud. If you think the temptation of receiving a large insurance check is too tempting for you, authorize the assignment of benefits. Of course, if you plan on paying out of pocket, you need not sign the assignment of benefits, and the insurance company will send the check to you for reimbursement.

Secondary or Supplemental Insurance

If you have supplemental insurance, before it will pay any of the remainder of your bills you will be required to submit an EOB from your primary carrier, another claim form and another itemized bill. Without an EOB the supplemental carrier will not pay any portion of the remaining bill.

Many providers will only take responsibility for the primary billing, so you may want to request that they also bill the supplemental carrier. If they won't, bill them yourself to insure payment. Either way, make sure you follow up accordingly.

No Insurance Coverage

Many people do not have insurance; if you are among the uninsured, do what you can to obtain coverage. If you require medical care before you are covered there are ways to help you ease the burden of the costs.

Hospitals have personnel ready to assist you in obtaining state aid to offset some or all of the medical costs. You'll be aided in identifying the proper agency to help you as well as in the preparation of forms and other requirements to start the assistance. The hospital will then notify you if you have qualified for aid under any of the available agency plans.

If you fail to qualify for state assistance, set up an arrangement to pay the provider. You will be required to specify your financial status and they will probably set up a payment arrangement that meets your finances. If you have more than one bill you should ask the provider to combine them so you have only one to pay. Frequently, a single hospital visit will generate many different bills.

Approach this request professionally. The provider needn't establish a payment plan for you; it is being done to help you. If you fail to abide by the payment plan, the provider can call the entire bill due in full. If you persist in defaulting, you will have your bill placed with a collection agency, and in most cases it will appear on your credit report.

MEDICAID

If you are receiving government assistance, be certain to carry your medical identification card with you and present it to the provider at the time of service. Get your visits pre-authorized through your case worker, so he/she will be aware that there will be a claim on file. The provider must submit the bills and medical identification information to the state before payment is received. There is a time limit for the submission of the bill, so if you forget your card, make sure you get it to the provider as soon as possible.

Follow up on your claims with your case worker or social worker. The volume of bills processed by the government is quite extensive and many may slip through the cracks if they are not carefully followed up. If you followed the instructions, you should never receive a bill from the hospital, but in the event you do, turn it over to your case worker immediately so he/she can get it filed. These agencies are not always speedy, so don't waste time.

Personal Injury/Workman's Compensation

When medical assistance is required as a result of someone elses negligence, the provider should be informed of who will be responsible for satisfying the resultant bills. Certain cases of negligence may require the assistance of an attorney.

When you are injured as a result of negligence (work, stores, etc), an accident report detailing the incident should be prepared as quickly as possible. In cases where you may be unable to prepare such a report, obtain an attorney. Have all itemized bills sent directly to your attorney. Cases of personal injury usually take very long to settle and in the meantime, your medical indebtedness may result in the providers turning the bills over to a collection agency. If possible, you should try to pay the bill out of pocket to avoid this, but if that isn't a feasible solution, inform the provider that you are represented by an attorney and that all correspondence must be sent to your legal representative. Your attorney will then request that the provider send a medical lien, which will guarantee payment upon settlement of the case.

Possible Changes in Health Care

The Federal Government is continually looking for ways to improve the health care system to enable more people to be covered and to make it more affordable. How these changes, if and when they occur, will effect the consumer is unknown, so we strongly recommend monitoring the various media outlets for developments.

As we've stated, no one asks for medical bills, but non-payment of these look just as bad on your credit history as reneging on a car note. Current bills that are being paid will not show up on your report and potential creditors could probably care less about them. But by not paying, they will more than likely show up on your credit report and have an impact on your ability to receive additional credit. Don't lose track of these bills; by taking care of them as you would any other bill, you will save yourself a lot of trouble in the future.

8

Mortgages and Credit

The largest purchase you'll make in your life will undoubtedly be your home. Before you can buy your dream house you'll probably need to have some kind of credit established to qualify for a mortgage. The mortgage process is very complex and requires time and effort on your part to be successfully concluded.

There are a variety of mortgage packages available and each requires considerable paperwork. You will have to furnish documents to substantiate income and, even if you have no previous loan or credit card history, you may be required to have your rent and utility payment history viewed in order to show your level of responsibility. The entire procedure is extremely time consuming and will only be compounded if you have problems on your credit report.

This chapter will discuss types of mortgages, where to get them, and the process involved that can help your chances of getting your mortgage approved in a timely fashion.

Types of Mortgages

Know what types of mortgages are available to you before deciding on a home purchase. The most popular loan package is the FIXED RATE MORTGAGE. This loan, usually extended for a 15 or 30 year period, will not fluctuate and your payments will not increase as mortgage rates go up.

Young professionals, first time home buyers, and people who relocate often might consider an ADJUSTABLE RATE MORTGAGE (ARM). This type of mortgage allows lower monthly payments for a few years, after which the interest rate is re-calculated based on interest rates at the time. It is possible that if rates go down, your payments may decrease. If rates go sky high, ARM's have a ceiling, or cap, which limits the amount the interest rate may change during each period and the life of the loan. There is also a cap on how much the payment may change.

A BALLOON MORTGAGE is a fixed rate mortgage that has a term of 5 to 7 years. You would pay small, regular payments during this period, but the loan matures at the end of the term, at which time the balance would be paid in full or the loan would need to be refinanced.

A BRIDGE LOAN is for someone who has found a new home but has yet to sell their old home. It is a short term arrangement that lenders scrutinize closely because of the obligations you would have to the current mortgage holder, the potential new mortgage holder, and the lender of the bridge loan, as well as normal monthly obligations.

JUMBO LOANS are loans that exceed the limits set by Fannie Mae and Freddie Mac (more on these two entities shortly), and have higher interest rates than traditional loan packages.

Builders of new homes can consider a CONSTRUCTION LOAN. This is a short term loan where the lender will advance funds to the builder as work progresses. The builder will then pay off the loan upon completion of the job.

FHA LOANS are insured by the Federal Housing Administration and are open to all qualified purchasers. There are limits on the size of FHA loans, but they are generous.

Veterans of military service may wish to pursue a VA LOAN, a long term loan guaranteed by the Department of Veterans Affairs, featuring low or no down payments.

Farmers and other qualified borrowers who are unable to obtain loans elsewhere may be eligible for an FMHA LOAN that is financed through the Farmers Home Administration.

If you know someone who owns a home you would like to purchase, you may also enter into a CONTRACT SALE with that person. You would agree to pay them a monthly payment toward ownership of the property.

Where to Look

We covered some of the types of mortgages available, but where should you begin your search? SAVINGS & LOANS (S&L'S) have long been a holder of mortgages. The loans are either funded by the institution using depositors money or sold in groups to investors and the secondary mortgage market.

This secondary market is basically made up of 3 companies regulated by the Federal Government: THE FEDERAL NATIONAL MORTGAGE ASSN. (FNMA), THE GOVERNMENT NATIONAL MORTGAGE ASSN. (GNMA), AND THE FEDERAL HOME LOAN MORTGAGE CORP. (FHLMC). These are better known as FANNIE MAE, GINNIE MAE, AND FREDDIE MAC, respectively. They buy groups of mortgages from various lending institutions, using money obtained from selling bonds and other investments, and provide money to the lenders to make additional mortgage loans.

Another traditional lender of mortgage loans are COMMERCIAL BANKS. As with S&L's, the loans are either funded by depositors money or sold to the secondary market. If funded and managed in house, commercial banks and S&L's will make money through the origination fees and interest.

MORTGAGE BANKERS serve as intermediaries between buyers and investors. The investors give the mortgage bankers money in exchange for a group of mortgages. They may also sell their packages to S&L's or commercial banks.

The initial capital to make the loans comes from a line of credit the banker has established with a major bank. The line of credit is paid off once the investors purchase the mortgages.

The newcomer to the mortgage game is the MORTGAGE BROKER. These brokers originate nearly half of all mortgage loans written. They bring the buyer and lender together by shopping the application. The broker does all of the paperwork and processing, then works with the lender to provide the best terms for the buyer. Once the application is accepted, the lender gives the money to the broker who turns it over to the buyer, thus ending his/her involvement. Brokers make their money through origination fees and money paid by the lenders.

The aforementioned are the main originators of mortgages, but smaller banks, credit unions, and private individuals can also be used as starting points for obtaining a mortgage.

The People in the Process

There are key people involved in the step-by-step process whenever you apply for a mortgage. The LOAN OFFICER is a person you will meet with face-to-face and will do everything possible to assist you in getting your mortgage approved. They will help you complete the application and discuss the different packages that are available. They will ask questions and request documents concerning your income, length of employment, and current liabilities. They may even "pull" a copy of your credit report and request additional information based on its contents.

The PROCESSOR handles the next step by organizing all of the information into your portfolio.

The person who will make the final decision on approval or denial is the UNDERWRITER. It is their responsibility to prevent bad loans that will prove to be unsalable to outside investors. They stay behind the scenes; the applicant will never have contact with the underwriter.

Mortgage Guidelines

Lenders generally have guidelines they follow before agreeing to finance a mortgage. A main concern is the borrowers ability to make the monthly payment, so ratios play an important role in determining eligibilty. The general rule of thumb for the HOUSING TO INCOME RATIO is that the mortgage payment should not exceed 28% of your gross monthly income, and the entire amount of the mortgage should not exceed

3 times your gross annual income on a 30 year mortgage (2 times for a 15 year mortgage).

The DEBT TO INCOME RATIO should generally not exceed 36% of your monthly gross salary. This ratio includes your mortgage payment plus all other liabilities you have incurred.

Don't be put off by these guidelines, however, because they are not set in stone. Lenders may make the ratios higher or lower depending upon varying circumstances. Buyers who may be up for a substantial promotion and raise may be allowed to exceed the lenders standard ratios now because they will come into line later. People who may be retiring soon may need to come in at lower figures.

Regardless of the situation, YOU must decide what will comfortably fit into your budget. You need to look ahead and determine what your financial future looks like and how it may change down the road.

Options are available, however. You may wish to purchase a less expensive house or request a lower ratio up front. You may choose to make a larger down payment which may allow a larger debt to income ratio; however, lenders don't like to see all available capital used for a down payment (they prefer a reserve of 3 months of mortgage payments). You may also ask about special programs that may available to assist people with similar circumstances. The important thing to remember is to take an active role in deciding how much of your budget should go toward housing.

Mortgage Credit Reports

Once the loan officer and applicant decide on a ratio, it may be necessary to get a credit report to outline outstanding liability, especially if the computation of debt-to-income will be close.

This is accomplished by contacting one of the many smaller credit reporting agencies that do specialized credit reports for mortgage lenders, landlords, rental agents, employers, and the like. This agency will access the databases of 1, 2, or all 3 of the big 3 credit bureaus using the personal information supplied by the loan officer. In return, the loan officer will get an INFILE OR PREQUAL, which is the raw credit from the bureau or bureaus. The report may contain duplicate tradelines, different information for the same accounts, and information that has not been recently updated.

The loan officer will then sift through this raw credit with you and determine whether to proceed or not with the application process. On occassion, you may need to furnish explanations or documentation on accounts that have not been updated or paid. The loan officer may also offer suggestions on accounts that need to be resolved before proceeding.

If the credit is clean or there are minimal problems and your explanations on questionable accounts are sound, the loan officer may decide to proceed, using the contents of your infile for your portfolio.

If there are problems or accounts need clearing, the loan officer may request a RESIDENTIAL MORTGAGE CREDIT REPORT, OR RMCR,from the credit reporting agency. Since a credit report, as well as other documents, must accompany every mortgage application, the RMCR will enable the questionable accounts to be cleared, updated, or deleted from your mortgage credit report. It also allows for removal of duplicate tradelines and the adding of manual tradelines, such as landlords and utility bills, to supplement existing credit or make up for lack of credit.

According to Fannie Mae and Freddie Mac guidelines, the RMCR must contain information obtained from at least 2 of the major credit bureaus. It must contain employment and residence information going back at least 2 years. It must contain any available public record information and all inquiries done within the last 90 days. All credit showing a balance cannot be more than 90 days old, but if it cannot be verified, a statement must be included on the report indicating that verification was not possible or was refused by the creditor. These are some of the things that Fannie Mae and Freddie Mac require. In addition, all credit reporting agencies doing RMCR's must abide by all laws of the Fair Credit Reporting Act (FCRA).

When the full RMCR is requested, it often means that there are some items that appeared on the infile that need to be taken care of. The processor working for the reporting agency can remove or correct items from the applicants credit report for the RMCR (with proper and sufficient documentation), but the guidelines in Chapter 5 must be followed to have corrections made on your permanent credit report.

The agency doing the RMCR will usually interview the applicant to assure that all of the credit appearing on the report is theirs and that all of the information they were given is accurate. The processor will then attempt to clear or verify anything that the applicant states is paid or erroneous.

If, after receiving the completed RMCR, the balances are still too high or adverse credit still shows as being unpaid, the loan officer may ask you to take care of the problem. When that has been done, the loan officer will request a SUPPLEMENT to the report, asking that the reporting agency only verify the questionable accounts and submit an updated report showing those items corrected.

How to Help Yourself

As we've stated, the mortgage process can be time consuming and, depending upon circumstances, it may take weeks to close on your loan. There are ways you can help speed up the process.

First of all, you should know what shows up on your credit report before your initial interview with the loan officer. If possible, get a copy of your report from all 3 credit bureaus, especially since you won't know which bureaus the mortgage company is going to be obtaining their credit from. Accounts that can be corrected should be. Explanations and documentation should be available for questionable accounts.

Paying off or paying down balances before the interview will shave days off of the process by not having to wait for payments to be posted. It should make it easier to meet the desired debt to income ratio.

If there are accounts that have been paid but are not being reflected as such (possibly collection accounts) you will be able to provide receipts showing that the payment was made. The same holds true for judgments and tax liens not being shown as satisfied. By knowing in advance how adverse credit is being reported, you can furnish the loan officer with proof up front.

If you filed for bankruptcy, the loan officer and credit reporting agency will need copies of the discharge papers and schedule of creditors included in the bankruptcy.

Do whatever the loan officer suggests, and do it immediately. If they ask for documentation, provide it as soon as possible. If they ask you to reduce debt or pay collection accounts, send the money next day delivery. If additional information is needed, give it to them. Remember, the longer it takes you to do the things they ask, the longer it's going to take for your loan to get approved.

Make yourself available to the loan officer and credit reporting agency. The loan officer may need to contact you after the interview and it's important that you call them back ASAP. You should also call the credit reporting agency if they leave a message. They wouldn't be calling if they didn't need information to clear something from your credit report, and failure to call back will delay completion of your RMCR.

Be honest on your application. Misleading information, whether accidental or intentional, may delay or halt the mortgage process, and fraudulent documents will most definitely lead to denial.

Understand the ratios, but remember that they are not etched in stone; they can be stretched.

Win the respect and trust of your loan officer; they work on commission and will help you in any way possible to obtain your loan. They are also responsible for "selling" your file to the underwriter, and it pays to have them on your side.

Shop around for a package that's right for you. Mortgage lenders are like any other creditor; they have different criteria for approval and different loans available.

Know what you can afford. Have a budget established and determine what you will comfortably be able to pay. Get involved in the entire mortgage process.

Check into special programs. Fannie Mae and Freddie Mac have programs available to first-time home buyers, and VA and FHA loans often offer special programs. You can also look into buying distressed or foreclosed on property, or lease with an option to buy.

Finally, monitor the media for who is offering the best rates and for changes in the mortgage process. For instance, both Fannie Mae and Freddie Mac are going automated, which will allow for approvals or denials within minutes in many cases.

Remember, the mortgage process is very complex and time consuming, take advantage of the things you are able to do to help speed up the process, and know what you will be able to comfortably afford to pay for your dream house.

9

Collection Agencies

The words "collection agency" and "bill collector" generally evoke negative and sometimes violent responses in people. No one wants to be harassed by a bill collector. If people would take the time to contact their creditors and try to work out their own payment problems, bill collectors wouldn't be necessary. When creditors have to resort to using bill collectors, the debtor becomes insulted and treats the collector like a thug and an unnecessary third party.

People generally use expletives to describe bill collectors. If you've ever been contacted by one you know what we mean. It is not, however, the bill collector who decided to take over your problem account. He has no voice in the matter. He cannot be blamed nor faulted for your credit problem. It is your fault only. It was your own negligence that led to the situation.

Bill collectors are not known to be pleasant people. Quite the contrary; they may be rude, annoying, loud and, occasionally, insulting. They never believe a thing you tell them. They send you nasty, "threatening" letters and call you at home and at work. They have a job to do and they do it. Remember, if you had taken care of the problem account by yourself, you wouldn't need to deal with a collector.

This is not a chapter praising bill collectors or the agencies they work for, but it is a chapter to make everyone aware of why we need them, how to deal with them, and your rights under the Fair Debt Collection Practices Act.

Why Creditors Use Collection Agencies

Every time a creditor turns a delinquent account over to an outside collection agency it costs the creditor money. Most creditors make an initial attempt to collect delinquent accounts themselves. All have in-house collectors, but their collection staff is usually small in size and are not always successful in their attempts. The outside agency has the time and means to effect a higher percentage of recovery on these difficult debts.

Many debtors just flatly refuse to pay their bills choosing, instead, to keep changing their addresses and phone numbers to avoid being caught by their creditors. Collection agencies use skip-tracing techniques to locate the debtors or, in this case, "skips". These techniques include contacting neighbors, friends, co-workers, and other creditors in an effort to locate the "skip".

In-house collectors can't devote the lengthy and concentrated amount of time to all the debtors the way an outside agency can. The great amount of collectors an agency has allows greater emphasis to be placed on each account.

The most cogent reason for collection agencies is the growing number of unpaid debts. As credit becomes more common and necessary, so does the need for debt recovery. The increase in bad debts has caused a concomitant surge in the growth of collection agencies. They are specialists in recirculating monies that would be lost otherwise.

What To Expect

Although some collection agencies relax their hostile efforts to recover money during hard economic times, when your account is turned over to an outside agency, you are no longer considered a customer. You have become a debtor, someone who owes money and has failed to honor the repayment agreements that were established. Don't expect the bill collector to treat you as though he were a customer service representative. The collector will treat you like the irresponsible person you've become. He won't believe a word you tell him as to why the debt has gone unpaid; he's heard every excuse there is several times over. Why tell him? You should have told the creditor about your problems before they got to this this level.

Any payment plan you may have arranged with the creditor will probably not be accepted by the bill collector; your balance will be due in full. If you can't pay it, you'll be told to borrow it and pay someone else back in monthly payments. The collector makes his money off these accounts, and monthly installments don't bring in large commissions. He feels that since you've reneged on your original installment agreement, why offer you another one? He will demand payment in full.

Some collectors may allow you to establish a monthly payment plan if your balance is quite large, but you will be asked to pay a substantial down payment as good faith money. If you are willing to make a large down payment, chances are good that you will continue to pay the remaining debt. Other collectors, if they have specific approval given them by their clients, may allow you to continue your original payment agreement as established by the creditor, but this is not the normal procedure.

As we indicated, the collector won't believe anything you say. You have to present irrefutable evidence to back up every statement you make to him. For example, if you were to say you already paid the creditor, you'd better have the cancelled check to prove it. You must be able to prove or substantiate what you tell the collector; this includes disputes, pending insurance claims, bankruptcies and billing errors.

The reason the shadow of doubt falls upon you stems from the account having been turned over to the agency. It has to be assumed that you don't want to pay your bill for if you did you would have made arrangements with the creditor long ago. With collection agencies YOU, THE DEBTOR, ARE ASSUMED GUILTY UNTIL YOU PROVE YOUR OWN INNOCENCE. You can expect the collector to make you feel guilty.

The collector may even try to make you feel like a thief. He'll tell you that charging merchandise and then not paying the bill is the same as stealing. He'll make you feel guilty about obtaining hospital treatment and services and then not paying the bill. He'll mention over and over that you are no longer a customer or a patient but, instead, a debtor.

You'll be told that your credit will be permanently tarnished until the bill is paid and that if it isn't paid immediately he'll recommend that his client (your former creditor) take "further action" against you. He'll make you feel bad and guilty regardless of your financial condition, and no excuse you give will make any difference. For every excuse you throw forth the collector has a counter response. The entire discussion will be directed toward establishing your guilt and inferring that if you don't pay immediately worse things will occur.

Most collection agencies rely on letters and phone calls to inform you of their involvement in the collection of your debt. Very few agencies have door to door collectors; more on all of this to follow.

The preceding paragraphs should have given you a good idea of what you could expect should an account of yours be turned over to a collection agency. It can be a humbling experience. Any person who has dealt with an agency knows the sick, frightening or hostility-provoking feelings evoked by the collectors. Those of you who have never been contacted by one are not missing anything good, and should work hard at keeping your credit accounts out of their hands.

The Dun

When your creditor realizes all his attempts to collect your bill have failed, he'll send one final notice. This letter will inform you that increased collection activity will follow if your account is not settled immediately. When you ignore this letter, your account will be turned over to a collection agency. Now the nasty letters begin.

The first letter you receive from the agency is called the first demand. This DUN, as all collection letters are called, gives all the pertinent information of who you owe the money to, how much you owe and it demands that you pay in full.

Additionally, and by law, it states that you have thirty days to dispute the validity of the bill, IN WRIT-ING, and request the name of the original creditor. The collection agency is identified by name, address and telephone number.

Failure to respond to this initial dun results in other duns being mailed, usually about every 2 weeks. Each one demands payment in full. The word-ing of each successive dun is more severe and infers that your failure to pay may result in asset investiga-tions and the recommendation to the creditor that "further action" should be taken against you. Some duns give you 72 hours to pay, others are indefinite on the time. All are abrupt and threatening.

The threat of further action means that if the col-lector can't get you to pay your bill, and if the agency has good information on where you work, and if you make more than $5 per hour and work full time, and if the creditor gives his approval, and if your debt is large enough to warrant, you will be sued. A lot of ifs are involved in the threat of "further action". It can, however, occur.

In addition to the scare duns, there are others that give or request information. They may ask for insur-ance information, proof of payment, notify you of broken arrangements, bounced checks, insufficient payments. An agency may use 20 to 30 form duns . . . one to serve any problem or situation. How many you receive depends upon the dollar amount of your bill and the creditor. Higher dollar amount debts usually receive more duns. Smaller debts, fewer duns. Why should the agency spend a lot of money on postage and letters when what you owe is not enough to cover the collection materials? Be informed, however, that the wording on these duns can be, and usually is, misleading and false; there use is primarily for purposes of intimidation.

YOU SHOULD ENDEAVOR TO CLEAR UP THE ACCOUNT UPON RECEIVING THE FIRST DUN. The longer the account remains open, the worse the situation may become. Respond to the first demand, attempt to make arrangements and stick to them if they are approved. If the bill is in error, take advantage of your legal right to request proof the the debt. Mail your dispute letter, certified mail, within the 30 allowable days after receiving the first demand. After thirty days, your dispute need not be honored although it may still be valid.

The Phone Calls

In addition to the duns, the agency will also contact you by telephone. The collector can call you anytime between the hours of 8 A.M. to 9 P.M. Monday through Saturday. The collector can call you at home, at work or leave messages that he called (in certain special instances) with your neighbors. THE COLLECTOR CANNOT CONTACT YOU MORE THAN ONCE A DAY. This means that if he leaves a message for you at your job, he can't then attempt to contact you at home, unless you give him permission to do so. YOU CAN BE CALLED EVERY DAY EXCEPT SUNDAY.

Since many of the articles in the FAIR DEBT COLLECTION PRACTICES ACT (FDCPA) are concerned with telephone calls from collectors, we've devoted a separate section to it.

What You Should Do

The most important thing you can do when dealing with bill collectors is KEEP YOUR COOL. Stay calm and do not lose your temper. Collectors are used to dealing with irate, hostile people; they do not back down but begin to push harder. If you keep your composure the collector will have a more difficult time dealing with you.

As we've previously mentioned, any time you re- mit a payment you should include your account num- ber on your check. Creditors make mistakes; periodi- cally payments are applied to the wrong accounts. If this has happened and, as a result, your paid account has gone to collections, retrieve a copy of the check or money order used to pay off the account and send it immediately to the collection agency. Let the collec- tor know the account was paid and tell him you will send the proof of payment certified mail.

If you already have a cancelled check that was used to pay the bill make a copy (front and back) and mail it to the collector. A money order copy can be obtained from your original place of purchase and mailed in. After you mail the collector the proof, call the creditor and complain that the account has been listed in error; demand that they remove it from col- lection and follow up on your demand to see that it was done. Also, if it was placed on your credit report, demand that it be removed immediately. It should be the responsibility of the creditor to see that it is removed even if it was placed on the report by the collection agency. Get a letter from the creditor or collection agency stating that the collection account should and will be deleted.

People forget to pay bills for any number of reasons. If you find that you have forgotten to pay a bill now in collection, pay it immediately to the collection agency. The bill must be paid in full. MAKE THE CHECK PAYABLE TO THE CREDITOR, but MAIL IT TO THE COLLECTION AGENCY. Do not send the money to the creditor; to do so will only delay a cessation of collection activities.

Collection agencies may or may not report to a credit bureau, and the only way to find out is to ask. The agency may not tell you so we suggest you assume they do. Please note that the agency is not required to notify the bureau of any payments you may be making on the account, only the original collection amount and a zero balance after the debt is paid in full. For this reason you must pay the bill, in full, as quickly as possible. If you cannot pay the bill in full DO NOT GO TO THE CREDITOR AND ASK FOR A MONTHLY PAYMENT ARRANGEMENT . . . YOU'LL ONLY BE SENT BACK TO THE COLLECTION AGENCY. You are going to have to try to arrange a payment plan with the collector, which is no easy task. You will usually be required to pay from 1/3 to 1/2 of the bill immediately to show good faith before being set up on a payment plan for the remainder. The bill would have to be large for the collector to agree to payments, so expect to make a large down payment.

If you don't have the amount of money the collector needs to arrange a payment plan try to borrow it from a friend or relative. If they don't have it, seek a debt consolidation loan. Don't hesitate; start looking immediately. If you are refused the loan get the company to give you a letter of denial and go somewhere else. Usually, when you can furnish a collection agency with proof that you have sought loans and were denied, they may be more willing to allow you a payment plan in retiring the debt.

Collectors sometimes will allow you to enter into a payment arrangement; other times, regardless of what proof you offer, a payment arrangement will not be allowed. Be aware that any money you send in must be credited to your debt. It is against the law to refuse your money (prior to legal action). A collector will usually tell you that your payments will not prevent the RECOMMENDATION of legal action against you, but rarely will suits follow if regular payments are mailed in to the agency. If you are taken to court you may be able to beat the suit by proving that you had faithfully sent in the most you could afford on the debt in a regular payment pattern.

Whenever you have legal representation involving a bill that is in collections, give the name and number of your attorney to the collector and state that all future correspondence be addressed to your counsel. Prevailing law requires collection agencies to cease active collection of an account that has legal representation. Certified letters to the agency informing them of your counsel should be sent. The same holds true with insurance companies. By giving the collector someone else to call, he won't call you.

Always attempt to get the collector to offer you a settlement figure on paying off the debt. If you get a settlement offer and you have the money to pay what is requested, pay it immediately. If the money won't be available to you until later in the month in which the settlement was offered, ask if a post dated check is acceptable. If the answer is yes, mail it in immediately, but you must be able to honor the post date of the check, for if you call the agency and tell them the check will not clear your bank on that date, the settlement offer will be repealed and the debt amount will be due in full.

Keep a written record of who you talk to and when you talk to them when dealing with bill collectors. Also take notes on the content of each discussion you have with the collectors. Many agencies change collectors frequently, and a collector new to your debt may not know the content of the discussions that preceded his involvement in your case. By keeping accurate records of your interactions with the agency, you may be able to file complaints and suits against them if it is necessary.

Never lie to a bill collector. When you say you're sending the money, send in the amount you promised. Send checks that clear your bank. The longer the bill remains unpaid and the more frequently you're caught in a lie, the nastier the collection methods become, and the longer it may stay open (as opposed to paid) on your credit report.

The Fair Debt Collection Practices Act (FDCPA)

This Act was written to protect the debtor from abuse and harassment by bill collectors. Everyone should be knowledgeable of its intent and content. Prior to enactment, there were few laws in effect to control the bill collector's intensity when collecting a debt. You may have been called any time, day or night; you may have been threatened, sworn at and embarrassed by having your debt become public knowledge to anyone the collector wished to tell.

The passage of the FDCPA placed restrictions on how far the collector could go in getting you to pay the bill. The Act is meant to protect the debtor and place specific controls on collection agencies so the public good is served. Overzealous collection practices have been responsible for significant erosion of the family unit through divorce, the economic stability of persons through bankruptcy, and societal disruption through breakdowns and suicide.

THE LAW APPLIES ONLY TO THIRD PARTY COLLECTION ACTIVITIES AND NOT TO FIRST AND SECOND PARTY IN-HOUSE COLLECTIONS, and, because of its length, we will concentrate only on those items that you, the consumer, will need to know to protect yourself from dreaded bill collectors.

The Laws

Collectors can contact third parties to obtain information relevant to the debtor's whereabouts. The collector can't tell the person a he/she is attempting to collect a debt. The party must be told where the collector is calling from, if asked, but by name only, not by function of the organization. Third parties are anyone other than the debtor, the debtor's spouse and the debtor's attorney. However, if the third party requests, in writing, that the agency no longer contact them, the collector must cease contact with that party.

A collector can speak with a third party ONLY if the debtor has given expressed permission to do so verbally or in writing, unless the debtor is a minor. Third parties include ex-spouses, insurance companies, parents or translators.

Collectors must cease all collection activities against a debtor if that debtor is represented by an attorney in a case specifically involving the debt. If the attorney fails to respond to a collector's query as to the attorneys representation of the debtor within a reasonable amount of time, collection may resume. The attorney may give the collector permission to contact the debtor.

Collection letters or duns must be mailed in envelopes free of any symbols or sayings that can be perceived as being from a collection agency.

Collectors can call debtors at their jobs unless it is reasonable to assume they know it will get the debtor in trouble, or unless the debtor says not to IN WRITING.

The collector must cease contact with the debtor if the debtor WRITES to the collector saying to no longer call or send duns, nor contact other persons about this debt. The letter must be sent registered mail and can be written formally or informally.

(Such a letter will usually make the collection agency either sue you or place the debt on your credit report. Keep a copy of the letter you sent for your own records. You may wish to include a sentence stating how you plan on retiring the debt. The collector can then send one last notice indicating receipt of your letter and stating that they may request the creditor seek legal remedies against you, or agreeing to your repayment terms).

The collector cannot harass, intimidate, or threaten you, nor use obscene or offensive language when speaking with you. The collector cannot lie about suing you, arresting you, or act as an attorney or an officer of the law or courts. (Use your common sense and listen to what the collector has to say. If it sounds less than legal to you, hang up and get assistance on whether you should proceed against the collector, but REMEMBER TO TAKE NOTES).

The collector MAY contact your neighbors in attempt to obtain information about you, but only if they have no working phone number by which to reach you.

The agency MUST submit a written notice (DUN) verifying that the debt is owed. This notice must give the amount of the debt, the name of the creditor, a statement explaining that the debtor has 30 days to dispute the validity of the debt or said debt will be considered valid, and a statement explaining that if the debtor does dispute the bill within the 30 day period, the collector will obtain verification of the debt and forward a copy on to the debtor, and cease collection activity until such time as the debtor receives the verification. (If the dispute DOES NOT come within the 30 period, collection activity is not required to cease).

It is unlawful for an agency to do any of the following: deposit a post-dated check before the listed date; fail to notify a debtor that a post-dated check is going to be deposited (if dated more than 5 days prior); place collect calls to debtors; or threaten to take any action that cannot legally be taken.

In the event of multiple debts, all money that is paid MUST be applied according to the wishes of the debtor.

These are the laws that are most often disregarded by bill collectors and the agencies that they work for. They were written to protect you from the intimidating tactics of some bill collectors, and ARE NOT included here to show how to avoid paying your bills, but as a way to preserve your human dignity.

Complaints and Suits

Whenever you feel that a collector has gone too far in trying to collect a bill, you may wish to file a complaint with the Federal Trade Commission or Attorney General. Write a letter specifying what rights of yours have been violated or laws compromised. Send a copy of the letter to the original creditor and to the collection agency. Include, when possible, specific laws that have been violated, and list incidents by names, dates and times of occurrence.

Indicate why the bill was delinquent and what you attempted to do to settle the account. Many times, a collection agency will set you up on payments rather than risk the scorn of the FTC, or their client (your former creditor) may order them to accept your payments or pull the account from them.

However, if you can prove beyond a doubt that the agency in question violated the law, you may want to hire an attorney and sue the agency. In addition to proving unfair practices, though, you will have to prove that an honest effort was made to resolve the matter. Chances of victory are good because even though the collector has a right to collect the debt, it doesn't give him the right to unduly harass you.

Even though some agencies will remove adverse information from your credit report upon payment of the bill in full, this is not the usual procedure. The account can legally remain there for 7 years, for all potential creditors to see, so avoid having collection accounts appear on your credit report. Take care of business and you will stay clear of these obnoxious collectors who work in America's collection agencies.

10

Bankruptcy

Deep and oppressive debt puts a person into a feeling of complete hopelessness. When you think you can't extricate yourself from the bills you believe you have no way of paying, your mind may drift toward thoughts of BANKRUPTCY.

Bankruptcy is as American as apple pie and hot dogs . . . isn't it? NO. BANKRUPTCY CAN BE A LONG-TERM SENTENCE TO CREDIT OBLIVION. It's something that you, if you're thinking about it, need to discuss with a financial advisor before seeing an attorney.

Bankruptcy attorneys will convince you that it is an effective way to get peace of mind. Most attorneys will make a weak, initial attempt to talk you out of it. Then, they'll discuss the cost and your legal rights to enter bankruptcy.

We suggest that you THINK LONG AND HARD BEFORE FILING.

Chapter 13

CHAPTER 13 falls under the Federal Bankruptcy Act and is a court approved plan to repay your creditors in monthly payments. Formerly called THE WAGE EARNERS PLAN, at one time a person was required to have a " . . . steady and sufficient employment income" before filing. Now, the law has been expanded to cover persons living on alimony or other forms of regular income. The income must be enough to allow the courts to approve a payment plan, usually running three to five years in length.

If your bills are very extensive you may be allowed to enter a "compensation plan" where a set percentage of your unsecured obligations are paid over a period of time exceeding the standard number of years.

There are no debt limits for wage earners, but for those whose income is derived from other than a regular paycheck (commission sales, brokering, etc.) a person cannot have debts exceeding $100,000 unsecured and/or $350,000 secured. This Plan is not intended to aid the poor but, instead, to help middle and upper middle income families who would forfeit assets by filing for personal bankruptcy.

Your attorney will tell you that your payment plan will be proposed to your creditors at a hearing established by the courts. The plan is voluntary and NO CREDITOR CAN FORCE YOU TO CHANGE IT; they can take it or leave it. If they leave it, they CANNOT ATTEMPT TO COLLECT THE DEBT; it will merely be discharged by the court, with the exception of alimony or long term secured obligations.

After approval, a court appointed trustee will oversee payment of monies to the creditors. Payments must begin within 30 days. Creditors have six months to file their claims after notification of the action by the courts, and must furnish proof that the debt is owed; failure to do so results in the claim being rejected. Those creditors who don't file will lose the right to collect their money.

Chapter 13 protects the debtor in ways other than by merely getting the bills paid. ALL COLLECTION ACTIVITIES AND LEGAL ACTION MUST CEASE. Correspondence from your covered creditors must go through your attorney. No more late fees, interest charges, or service fees are allowed. In addition, cosigners are offered the same protection as you are under this plan.

You will be able to retain all of your assets under the plan. Property cannot be repossessed nor can liens be placed against your assets, although nothing can be sold or paid without the courts consent. Your landlord, however, may still receive court permission to seek an eviction order.

Chapter 13 doesn't stigmatize a debtor. Most creditors will not be frightened away by a person who shows a discharged Chapter 13 on their credit report. Creditors will realize that the debtor has paid all of the debts, not cancelled them through a personal bankruptcy. Be warned, however, that failure to make the payments will result in the plan being dissolved or dismissed, at which time the creditors may resume any action that was being taken against you prior to the filing. If, for some reason, you are unable to complete your plan, the trustee may modify your plan, or you may switch to a Chapter 7, provided you haven't completed such a plan within the previous 6 years.

Personal Bankruptcy

CHAPTER 7 is BANKRUPTCY IN ITS TRUE FORM. An attorney will detail all your outstanding bills and file a petition with the Courts to discharge your debts. Your creditors will have the opportunity to express their objections to discharging the debts but most do not, unless they believe the amount of their bill is too large to let go without a fight.

Following this hearing, the judge will order the creditors to a second hearing at which their lists of debts must be presented. The final step has the court ordering the sale of your nonexempt assets, the proceeds of which will be used to pay your creditors. Your nonexempt assets vary from state to state, but they are, basically, assets other than your car, up to $7500 interest in property and several other things better described by your attorney. The process takes 3 to 6 months to complete, but generally only requires one trip to court.

When and if the Court approves the petition, you will be freed of your listed debts with the exception of any alimony or child support ordered, taxes owed that are less than three years old,student loans less than 7 years old, DUI judgments, a loan of any age acquired through fraudulent means, or improper conversion of encumbered assets (cars and stereos) when money is still owed to the creditor.

Disadvantages of Filing Bankruptcy

Your ability to get credit following personal bankruptcy is greatly impaired. Most persons feel little or nothing at having had to file and, as a result, may not have learned from their past mistakes. The same mistakes may be repeated, leaving the creditor open to seize your property when you fail to make your payments; you won't be eligible to file another personal bankruptcy, and chances are slim that attempting to file a Chapter 13 will be successful. Also, as we've mentioned previously, a Chapter 13 can remain on your credit report for 7 years, a Chapter 7 for as long as 10 years.

Re-Establishing Credit After Bankruptcy

As mentioned, filing a Chapter 13 instead of a Chapter 7 bankruptcy could make it much easier to get back on your feet after filing. Since a Chapter 13 requires repayment, many creditors are not as gun shy about extending credit to an applicant showing a discharged Chapter 13 on their credit report. This is not, however, a guarantee.

There are a few things you will need to do before before appplying for credit. First, get a copy of your credit report. This is important because there is a good chance that it will not reflect your bankruptcy as being discharged, nor will it show which creditors were included as part of the bankruptcy. You will probably need to send the bureau or bureaus a copy of your discharge papers and a schedule of creditors to have your report updated (be sure to have them send you a new report after it is updated).

The next step is to re-think your budget. You don't want to make the same mistakes that caused the bankruptcy, so begin a savings plan.

Finally, apply for a secured credit card or loan. Take some of the budgeted money for savings and deposit it in a bank that will issue you a secured card or loan. The savings account will act as collateral.

It's not easy to get back on your feet after a bankruptcy. The important thing is that you don't make the same mistakes twice. Learn that credit is something that should not be taken lightly.

Bankruptcy Abuse and Fraud

As we've mentioned previously, your creditors do have the right to challenge your bankruptcy, and some credit card companies have retained attorneys just for this purpose. What these attorneys are looking for are cases of bankruptcy fraud, which carry severe penalties.

BANKRUPTCY FRAUD is hiding assests or over-stating expenses; it's living above your means then filing bankruptcy to avoid having to pay your bills; it's lying about your income on credit applications, or using someone elses social security number to receive credit. But most important, it's a possible fine and imprisonment if you get caught.

Bankruptcy is a costly endeavor, both financially and psychologically. The stress of filing generally continues for years after the act. YOU MUST CONSIDER THIS CONTINUED EFFECT OF BANKRUPTCY BEFORE YOU ENTER IT. TRY EVERYTHING AND ANYTHING ELSE FIRST.

11

Creditor Action

As we have mentioned before, negative remarks on your credit report will have a huge impact on your ability to obtain additional credit. Should you default on the payment arrangements specified for your contracts, your creditors can take several courses of actions against you. Once these actions are instituted, they will not only appear on your credit history, they may stay with you for as long as seven years.

Creditors will usually threaten you with these actions before they invoke them. This is because the actions are both costly and time consuming. Creditors would rather work with you in resolving these problems rather than implement legal action against you . . . but they will if you fail to respond to their initial demands.

You must be notified whenever any legal action is instituted. If you receive such a notice make a last attempt to work out the problem. When this fails, hire a good attorney and begin preparing your defense against the action.

Repossession

REPOSSESSION is the seizure of goods, that you have purchased or pledged as collateral, when you renege on your payment agreements. The creditor has the right to take back the merchandise and sell it to obtain recompense for the balance that is in default. Is it as easy to do as it sounds? It can be, as in the case of an auto. The creditor can have a "Repo Man" "pull" the car from your driveway or parking space at work. They can take it at noon or at midnight; the creditor has a right to his property.

What if we're talking about a television. The creditor can't break into your house and take it . . . can he? No! If you don't want to give up the merchandise tell the "Repo Man" to get lost. He can't threaten or intimidate you, nor in any way breach the peace when attempting to repossess the property. If you want to keep it, you can, at least until the creditor obtains a court order to retrieve the merchandise.

If you don't want to fight the repossession then let the merchandise be taken. Once the creditor gets possession of the property, it will be sold to pay off the outstanding amount of the debt, although any difference, or deficiency balance, will still be your responsibility to pay.

Merchandise that has been pledged as collateral can be taken in the same way, but institutions that have allowed you to put up merchandise for loans received would rather have your payments than possession of your personal goods. These lending institutions may decide to garnish or attach your wages instead of seizing and selling your property.

Foreclosures

FORECLOSURES are similar to repossessions but deal with property such as homes, businesses, acreage; a court order is required. Foreclosures are a very costly process and every effort should be made to satisfy your mortgage payments to prevent the action.

A notice of foreclosure does not necessarily mean that you would have to immediately vacate your home or business property. Some states allow a party to continue living in the home for a set period of time, and even retain possession of the property when missed payments are fulfilled.

Wage Garnishments

The legal process by which a creditor gets a court order requiring your employer to withhold a percentage of your pay and pay it to that creditor is called a WAGE GARNISHMENT or ASSIGNMENT. The maximum amount legally withheld varies from state to state, with some states disallowing the action entirely.

After obtaining a JUDGMENT through the courts, you are notified that a wage attachment is imminent and that you have been granted the right to have a hearing to explain your situation. This first notice serves also as a warning and attempt to motivate you to pay the debt. Failure to respond results in the issuance of a second notice to you and your employer.

Failure to respond to this second notice will result in the assignment being enforced; your employer will have no say in the matter. Once the order is effected it will continue until the debt has been paid in full or until your decide to quit your job and/or file bankruptcy.

You cannot be terminated (in most states) because you have had your wages attached. The process will probably make you appear irresponsible to your employer and could result in fewer offers of promotion coming your way.

In the event that a judgment or TAX LIEN, which is a claim against your property for non payment of taxes, does appear on your credit report, make sure, once the obligation is satisfied (paid in full), that it is released through the courts. Failure on your part to do this will result in the disposition of the judgment or lien showing not satisfied, as opposed to satisfied. Your attorney will be able to assist you in getting the release papers filed. This will not be grounds to have the item removed, but only to have the disposition reflect that the obligation has been met.

Judgments that were vacated or dismissed by the court should not appear on your credit report. If they do, demand that they be removed and offer the court papers as proof.

The bottom line is this: take care of business and don't give your creditors the chance to beat you in court!

12

Credit and the Media

Credit is a big business, with millions of dollars at stake each year, and because of this, things are constantly changing. As competition increases, credit card companies offer more benefits to their cardholders. Marketing wizards of major corporations are discovering the gold mine that exists by offering a bank card with additional perks, such as the GM Mastercard. The government has also gotten on the credit bandwagon by offering to allow people to pay their taxes with their credit card. Many police departments are realizing that with so many speeders carrying plastic, it makes sense to let them pay their tickets with a credit card and be on their way. Credit card companies justify these changes as part of a transition to what they forsee as a "cashless society" where there is no need for cash transactions.

Because of these and many other changes, it would be impossible for us to continually update this publication, but you can keep abreast of what is happening in the world of credit just by reading the paper, listening to the radio, or watching television. Credit is news and news is what the media deals in. Call it what you will-consumer credit, personal finance, consumer spending-it will be reported by the various media outlets.

Many newspaper business sections carry credit items that will be of interest to the consumer. Some Sunday papers will have an entire section devoted to consumer and money issues, including where to get the best rates on credit cards or mortgage loans and where to obtain secured credit cards. Television often airs programs on consumer finance, and specials on consumer fraud and how to protect yourself from it can frequently be seen on the nightly news. Even watching television commercials can give you a lot of information about what is going on in the credit world. There are also publications aimed directly at consumers that contain articles and information about consumer credit, such as Money magazine.

Below are a few credit tidbits that we have come across while writing The Credit Jungle. These have come from all available media sources and are all true. As can be seen, most are very informative.

A. According to the National Center for Financial Education, approximately 33% of all credit reports on consumers contain inaccurate information (although we believe the figure is probably much higher). Remember to check your credit report at least once a year.

B. The number of personal bankruptcies in the U. S. has more than doubled since 1981, according to the American Bankruptcy Institute, and is expected to jump substantially in the next few years.

C. Winnebago County, Illinois jail officials have recently started accepting Visa and Mastercard as payment of bail for prisoners.

D. Many groups that monitor telemarketing fraud are now beginning to realize that those 900 numbers offering to clean up your credit or give you loans are nothing but scams aimed at people looking for a way out of their credit troubles.

E. The Consumers Union, which publishes Consumer Reports, is urging Congress to get more involved with the credit reporting process and force them to clean up their files.

F. A tax simplification bill has been endorsed by the Senate. Part of the bill allows taxpayers to pay their taxes with their credit cards.

G. In Illinois, 9 loan brokers, those "loans by mail regardless of your credit history" companies, were charged with numerous violations by the Illinois Attorney General due to numerous complaints received from the public.

H. Two companies offer various lists for those shopping for credit cards. For more information, write to Bankcard Holders of America at 560 Herndon Pkwy. Suite 120 Herndon, Va. 22070 or RAM Research's CardTrack at PO Box 1700 Frederick, MD. 21702.

I. The U. S. Supreme Court gave individuals the right to file bankruptcy under Chapter 11, with provisions that are usually used by ailing corporations to pay off their creditors over time.

J. According to a recent Gallup Poll, 63% of all Americans are afraid that they are currently too deep in debt.

K. People's Bank of Connecticut and the nations largest Hispanic television network, Telemundo Group Inc., are introducing a new bilingual credit card.

L. Citibank has cut interest rates for its best customers, a move that is taking place because of the increased price wars in the credit card business.

M. Optima Card, a subsidiary of American Express, is taking the lower interest rate idea one step further. It will offer different rates to different customers depending only upon their credit record or charge volume.

N. In an effort to cut down on credit card fraud, Citibank has introduced credit cards with pictures on them.

O. In Ohio and Texas, an incentive program is in effect to encourage people contemplating bankruptcy to file a Chapter 13 instead of a Chapter 7. The program basically promises the consumer that creditors will consider extending them new credit once they complete the repayment plan. The program has been a success in both states.

P. It is now possible to buy groceries with your credit card.

Q. Mastercard, Visa, and American Express are competing for customers in newly industrialized nations such as Poland.

R. The FTC, concerned over consumer privacy issues, is trying to stop TRW and TransUnion from using its consumer information for mailing lists.

S. TRW will team with Grupo CIS to form a credit reporting agency in Mexico. The new company, called Comcred, is expected to begin operations in 1995.

These are only a few of the many items on credit and the consumer that we have located, and each item goes into much more detail than we have included here. The important thing to remember is that this information affects you, the consumer, and you should be aware of it. Many things that we have not mentioned here but have noted in the main text of the book, such as changes in credit reporting procedures or the health bill, will affect you directly, so we suggest you keep your eyes and ears open to news on these changes.

As we stated in Chapter 5, both the House and Senate passed separate amendments to the Fair Credit Reporting Act, although an agreement was never reached on a total change to the FCRA. We strongly urge all people to monitor the media for information on these changes and the effect it will have on consumers.

Other information that can have a bearing on credit and may be of interest to you are mortgage rates (for the home buyer), finance charges for new cars (for the car buyer), and stores that offer no interest charges for a length of time (for those shoppers looking for a bargain). All of these items can have an effect on your credit situation, and all can be found in the various media outlets. Once you know what information you're seeking, gathering the information is as easy as reading the newspaper or other trade publications, watching television, or listening to the radio. Try it and see.

13

The Five Important Acts

We have referenced many Federal Laws in the text of this book. These laws were enacted by the government to protect you, the consumer.

Following are what we believe to be the five most important CONSUMER PROTECTION ACTS and a synopsis of what each covers.

The EQUAL CREDIT OPPORTUNITY ACT entitles you to equal credit consideration regardless of race, sex, age, color, religion or marital status. It does not guarantee you credit; it does protect you from discrimination in your quest for credit, and requires creditors to explain reasons for denial of credit.

The TRUTH IN LENDING ACT requires creditors to reveal the annual and monthly interest rates and minimum monthly payments for their credit structures.

Credit Bureaus are covered under the FAIR CREDIT REPORTING ACT. This act allows you access to your credit report as well as the ability to dispute and clarify inaccurate and negative information appearing on it.

You are protected from harassment and threats from collection agencies under the FAIR DEBT COLLECTION PRACTICES ACT. The FAIR CREDIT BILLING ACT protects you against erroneous billing, allowing you 60 days to notify a creditor, in writing, if you believe your bill is in error; it allows the creditor 90 days to correct or justify the bill.

To obtain copies of the complete acts check your local library or contact the Federal Trade Commission in Washington,D.C. Regional offices in the following cities should also be able to help you: Atlanta, Boston, Chicago, Cleveland, Dallas, Denver, Los Angeles, New York, San Francisco and Seattle.

Should you feel that any of your rights have been abridged contact your State's Attorney Generals Office or the FTC.

Conclusion

The Credit Jungle is a consumers guide to credit. It was written because of the numerous people who needed assistance in establishing, maintaining, or cleaning up their credit. These people came to us with their concerns and were the inspiration for this book, and we thank them.

The various Acts that we have cited throughout this text were written to protect you, the consumer, but the average person has no idea of what his/her rights are in regards to consumer credit. These laws are set up to ensure that you are treated fairly in all aspects of credit; whether you are just establishing your credit, dealing with bill collectors, or trying to have an erroneous item removed from your credit report, you must learn to use these consumer protection laws to your advantage.

We've taken these laws and put them into a handy reference guide, and all you need to do is follow our guidelines. We can't do it for you, but we can show you the methods that will get the best results, and everything in The Credit Jungle has proven to be effective.

It all comes down to determination. While you're in the market for your first home is no time to be thinking about your credit situation. THE TIME TO START DOING SOMETHING ABOUT IT IS NOW!!!

Just remember, there are two ways to do everything, and selecting the wrong way, especially in the credit society, can mean the difference between a happy, prosperous life and a life of worry and frustration. Your credit, good or bad, is for life, and only you can decide what's best for you. Remember that once you start out on your chosen path, it's a long way back to the starting point if you see you've made the wrong choice.

So be responsible; use your credit wisely and you'll have an easy time conquering . . . THE CREDIT JUNGLE.